"Jesus Chr[ist]

May the Peace & Jehovah God reign down on you!

From:

Pastor Helen

Fear not [there is nothing to fear]. for I am with you; do not look around you in terror and be dismayed, for I am your God, I will strengthen and harden you to difficulties, Yes, I will help you up and retain you with My [victorious] right hand of rightness and justice

Isaiah 41:10

God bless you!

Breaking Through My Invisible Bubble

by

Helen Patricia Rolle Rahming

AuthorHouse™
1663 Liberty Drive, Suite 200
Bloomington, IN 47403
www.authorhouse.com
Phone: 1-800-839-8640

©2008 Helen Patricia Rolle Rahming. All rights reserved.

No part of this book may be reproduced, stored in a retrieval system, or transmitted by any means without the written permission of the author.

First published by AuthorHouse   9/18/2008

ISBN: 978-1-4343-4724-4 (sc)
ISBN: 978-1-4343-6901-7 (hc)

Printed in the United States of America
Bloomington, Indiana

This book is printed on acid-free paper.

Photographs by Agatha Christie
www.jcimagebahamas.net

Definitions taken from Merriam Webster's Collegiate Dictionary. Tenth Edition.
Scripture taken from the Amplified Bible Copyright c 1954, 1958, 1962, 1964, 1965, 1987 by The Lockman Foundation. Used by permission.

Helen P. Rolle Rahming
P.O. Box EE-15720
Nassau, Bahamas

hidingplace7@yahoo.com

Dedication

The Lord Jesus Christ, who loves me so much that He shed His precious blood for me.
My children:
Edrick Neil Cleare and his wife Kimberley, Dr. Heatherlyn Patrona Hoffman and her husband Dr. Louis, Earnal DeMorbelle Cleare, Ambrozino Lecaster Storr and his wife Jennifer, who encouraged and gave me the motivation to write this and many more books and to not let anything or anyone get in the way of my spiritual walk with Jehovah God and my passions.

Thanks, children, for believing that I have the potential to achieve greatness, and for telling me whenever we speak, "I love you very much." I deeply appreciate your listening ear, words of wisdom filled with spiritual nuggets, financial support when necessary, and words of encouragement, as you daily push me up the ladder through your inspiration that I can do it:

"The sky is the limit; forget about your age — it's never too late."

You have touched my life with your individuality that made me come alive with laughter even though your teasing at times is a bit harsh, while respecting my position always as your mother.

To my grandchildren, DeMeo, Aaron, MeKel, Ambranette, Ambrozino Jr., Lakoda, Kamerin and Kharis. Just your smiles, hugs and kisses bring much joy into my heart.

I am grateful to Almighty God and for the inspiration of the Holy Spirit to write this book, then to you my beloved children and grandchildren.

May grace, peace, and mercy abide with you always! Remain bonded together always in whatever areas of support that is needed.

May Jehovah God bless you and your generation to come in abundance! I love you.

Acknowledgements

To my husband, Rev. Theodore C. Rahming, with much appreciation, I thank you for the various contributions. May Jehovah God bless you abundantly with wisdom, knowledge and understanding as you continue to seek His face with all diligence and faithfulness! Do the work of the evangelist in the power of the Holy Ghost, to which you have been call to do.

To those whom I have taken under my wings as my own children, some of whom call me "Mom": Granville O'Brien, Theresa Guy and her husband Andrew, Thomasina Roberts, Sharon Knowles, Marsha Peters, Pastor Tamu McKinney, and Charlene and Ainsley Deleveaux. Thanks for your prayers and words of encouragement. I have watched you go after your passions with much vigor and I am inspired by you.

To my stepchildren, Kenva, Tekea, Adrian and Na-Amah, step-grandchildren Kendeira and Danielle, thanks for your contributions and may Jehovah God bless you.

To my other family members, especially my sisters, Albertha Davis, Willamae Sands and her husband Alvan, Creola Kelly and her husband Brudinell, Dorothy Springer, Nurse Bridgette Cash and her husband Paul, Emerald and Remilda "Millie" Rolle; my brothers, Sgt. Andrew Rolle and his wife Sandra, Supt. of Police, Kevin "Chick" Rolle and his fiancée Dr. Marsha Bethel, Blaise Rolle and his wife Serena, Peter Rolle and his wife Carmen, Keith Rolle; adopted brothers, Deacon Freddie Ramsey, and Larry Higgs.

To all those whom I call my adopted sisters, especially Deli whom I have known for thirty-eight years, and others too many to name. You know who you are and the individual contributions you have made in my life, and will be able to identify yourselves when you read this book.

There were moments when you unselfishly loaned me your shoulders to cry on or just had a listening ear. I didn't know that in my humility inside my relationships I was being an inspiration to you. I was reminded frequently to forgive and to let go and let God. I look back at other uncomfortable times that I encountered and was suddenly uplifted in spirit and know that at that very moment you were praying for my restoration and healing.

I will forever be grateful to you for your support in the areas of confidentiality, words of encouragement, financial support in many different ways such as, taking me to the nail parlor, giving me bags of groceries, a little envelope with a cute drawing of a lady dressed in a ball gown, and inside there was your contribution, a drive by my house just to extend your hand in mine leaving your donation, and a souvenir from your travels or your financial donations during my travels, and most importantly, your continued spiritual uplifting. Thank you.

To Apostle Dr. Douglas Cleare and Apostle Dr. Betty L. Cleare who mentored me for seventeen years.

To Pastors Winston and Parnell Barker.

To Sis. Deborah DeRosia.

To my cousin, Rev. Dr. Gloria Woods, who continues to mentor me!

To my pastors and mentors, Bishop Sheldon D. and Pastor Jennifer M. Newton of "Jesus Christ Centered Ministries International".

Thanks for your persistence in pulling the best out of me through your mentoring. May Jehovah God strengthen, bless, and under-gird you as you continue to fight the good fight of faith. May He continue to use you to lead others to the Lord Jesus Christ and to bring deliverance and healing to His people!

Again, thanks to all of the above from the depths of my heart. I love you.

Table Of Contents

The Weights 3

Remembering 15

The Awakening 35

The Breakthrough 39

The Cleansing Process 51

Pressing on with Thanksgiving, Praise, and Worship 71

His Voice 81

Conclusion 97

CHAPTER I

The Weights

The raging storm waters seemed to be stirring violently, deep within my soul, pressing and stretching every nerve endings, every cell and fiber of my entire being.

I closed my eyes, trying to drown out the negative sights and the awful feeling, but suddenly I felt as though I was losing my balance within my invisible bubble.

Feelings of doom and gloom quickly engulfed my soul.

I envisioned myself drowning and being found days later.

I saw myself purposely falling from a tall building.

There was also a quick glimpse of myself losing my mind as my skin began to feel as though something was crawling underneath it.

I would wrap my hands around my body to try to calm myself.

As the physical pain wracked my body the headaches became worse and the dizziness increased, causing me to almost lose my balance on several occasions.

There were periods of clenching fists and gritting of the teeth, racing heartbeat associated with panic attacks and anxiety.

The weights were too heavy for me to bear, and I needed to be freed from my grave clothes with much haste.

From deep down within, I tried to scream for help, but the sounds, which remind me of the dog whistle that can only be heard by dogs and not by the human ear, were not heard by those around me.

Here I am, trying to gain strength, stretching and flexing in all directions inside my invisible bubble, with tears flowing like melted ice from the side of a frozen bottle.

For the duration of time spent in my invisible bubble I remained courteous and cordial, so that the evidence of my depleted spiritual life would not be seen. It was a camouflage. But I knew, and those who were walking in the Spirit knew, too, that I was living a lie.

I would look in the mirror at myself and see a withdrawn person who seemed to just be withering away or dissolving like sugar in a glass of water.

Loss of appetite and sleepless nights resulted in my developing a nervous system, and fear gripped my body in an overwhelming manner.

Yes, I must rise. I must break forth like the sun peaking through the dark clouds, a ray of light here and there until I can see my way clear.

I must then follow the pathway, the way of escape from the dark energy that has tried so hard and so long to swallow me up or squeeze the very life out of me.

With constant tears flowing down my cheeks, and cries from within to the Holy Spirit, I said, ***"Help me. I don't*** *know what to do. You haven't brought me this far to leave me now."*

Negative laughter and whispers from the pit of hell seemed to be bombarding my invisible bubble, from the east, west, north, and south both day and night.

Persons of low degree and high degree looked at me in amazement. I was truly not the person they knew years ago who functioned under the unction of the Holy Spirit.

Was I imagining all this? Was I hearing things?

Much of my prayer life at that time was, *"Please Lord Jesus, do not leave me. I am weak and worn and I need you to undergird me with Your strength."*

Day by day, as situations arose and the dark energies surrounded me, the yokes seem to be getting tighter around my spiritual neck, suffocating the very life out of me.

My physical body began to see the manifestation of the weights as my body was continuously enveloped with pain and I felt claustrophobic. My spirit was indeed broken.

Yes, the storms of life were all around me, but I must hasten to escape from my invisible bubble before I was swallowed up like a prey caught off guard by its predator that swiftly snatched it from the wild.

The screen, which read **"pessimism,"** was sprawled open in front of me like a scroll, and there I saw myself as an unwanted child, followed by hopelessness and discouragement that crept slowly into my spirit from the many inner bruises, hurts, and wounds, and yes all the rejection.

To some it may have seemed as if I was covered with leprosy, as the stench of death was encased all around me, causing some to pass me by.

To others I was viewed as a well-groomed, sophisticated woman of excellence who had it made in the shade.

But on the inside where only the Holy Spirit could see, this once-powerful woman of God was filled with a dead man's bones and bore the inward scars from many years before and some present that was silently and secretly ingrained in my soul.

My head was bowed in shame. I was disgusted with myself.

The glory of God had surely departed, and my countenance had fallen. There were obvious signs of this, as those who walked in the Spirit would say, "Something is wrong with you. There is no smile on your used-to-be-jubilant face!"

My World Was Caving In

Philippians 4:13 (AMP) says,
"I have strength for all things in Christ Who empowers me [I am ready for anything and equal to anything through Him Who infuses inner strength into me; I am self-sufficient in Christ's sufficiency."

These were but mere words on the pages of the Christian Bible, as it seemed as though I was only going through the motions during this period.

My conscious mind seemed to be spinning like a merry-go-round, and my thoughts shook together like pieces of chicken in a bag of Shake 'n Bake.

My inner strength was quickly failing.

In the midst of the storms inside my invisible bubble, I began to think of the many gifts and talents that Jehovah God had blessed me with, but I heard voices that echoed from the pit of hell: "You will never get anything accomplished." "Where will you get the finances? You have no income!" "You need to find a job as your children will eventually get tired of you."

Misunderstandings again, I thought. Yet I knew deep within my heart that the visions and dreams that were given to me by the Holy Spirit would provide for me financially. Also, because of the binding relationship that my children and I have had for many years, I will always remain confident that they would not forsake me in my hour of need.

Words of encouragement came from here and there, but they seemed to dissipate among the loud and silent sounds from the negative voices.

The question arose, "Will I go to the land of the dead not fulfilling the purpose to which God has called me to with so much inner wealth that was never released, without leaving behind a legacy for my generation? Well, guess what? It surely didn't matter in those days.

My inner man cried,

"Help Me, Lord Jesus."

With so many plans on the drawing board, and doors not seemed to be opening, defeat seemed certain inside my bubble. Doom and gloom were the order of the day.

I feared tomorrow and the repeat of uncomfortable situations and circumstances that arose periodically, and sometimes too frequently, that included finances and health; and to top it all off my "soul" was not prospering.

3 John verse 2 (AMP) says,

"Beloved, I pray that you may prosper in every way and [that your body] may keep well, even as [I know] your soul keeps well and prospers."

Before I go any further, though, let me explain the meaning of the word *bubble*,

- *something (as a plastic or inflatable structure) that is hemispherical or semicylindrical;*
- *something that lacks firmness, solidity, or reality;*
- *a delusive scheme.*

This definition describes in detail the state of my foundation.

I was living in a world where I had no grip on life, and I was quite deluded, as I had experienced situations and circumstances in my relationships that I was in complete awe about. I was not anchored solidly to the **vine, Jesus Christ.**

Can you relate to this? We'll see as I go further.

The struggles seemed so insurmountable, as I was going through much hurt, pain, rejection, disappointment, and feelings of being unloved. I felt that relationships all around me were deteriorating at a fast pace, but I was persistent in breaking through my bubble with whatever strength I had left.

Saints, who knew me and the work that the Lord had done through me in times past for many years, prayed consistently for and with me for healing and restoration.

They spoke words of encouragement that brought back to my vivid imagination soothing memories.

I was in hot pursuit to escape from this dark dungeon that illuminated various demonic actions.

How much longer, Oh Lord? I am tired and weary, but I must press on to the road of victory, as I am being made a minister.

The Potter's hands were molding me, chiseling out all of the imperfections, smoothing out the rough edges, the gossiping, murmuring, complaining, anger, bitterness, hatred, etc., and carving me daily into what He wanted me to be.

Even Though It Hurts, Your Perfect Will Be Done, Father

I think of a fish being scaled and then cut open to remove its bowels. Salt and pepper are then placed inside and rubbed on the outside to give it seasoning that would be tasty for the palate.

As I write this biography, I know that the Potter is still working on me, not leaving a trace of anything that would hinder my spiritual growth any longer. The stench of sin, which had been lingering for many years, must be removed, including unforgiveness, bitterness, etc., and holiness and righteousness must now take up residence.

But at this crucial time in my life, I was walking in rebellion to God's word as I was too caught up in my hurts and wounds that had me blinded towards the road of my destiny. I was not really focusing on things that I had done but on things that had been done to me.

What should I do? Who should I turn to?

I Took My Eyes Off My First Love – The Lord Jesus Christ

It seemed as though regardless of which direction I took, east, west, north, or south — more anguish was brought on than I than I could bear, as misunderstandings arose from all sides.

The wind and the waves roared angrily, tossing me to and fro as a ship on the high seas, and I seem to be caught smack in the middle.

I thought that if I could only find the entrance to this invisible bubble, I would swiftly escape. But the weights that surrounded me were too heavy and too strong, and I became weak and felt pressed in from every side.

The spiritual chains tightened around my entire being like a hangman's noose around a prisoner's neck awaiting instruction for the chair to be removed.

During my time alone I would silently shed tears that would flow uncontrollably as I focused on past and present situations and circumstances in my life, doing so with much caution.

I would wrap my hands tight around myself, to control the nervousness.

If I screamed others would hear, and what would they think in the neighborhood?

Surely she must have gone crazy. She is surely insane! Some might have even volunteered to call the "bus" to take me away.

2 Timothy 3:11 (AMP):

"Persecutions, sufferings- such as occurred to me at Antioch, at Iconium, at Lustra, persecutions I endured, but of them all the Lord delivered me."

Would deliverance come to me soon before I slipped into the land of the dead?

I felt as though I was being boiled alive in a pressure cooker in which the ingredients it contained were those of persecutions, misunderstandings, and yes, hurts and wounds that were embedded in the marrow of my bones.

For many, many years I had succumbed to the ills of others in close relationships, and I was too blind to see that I was being controlled by their actions. This was mental and emotional abuse, and the spirit of control was being thrust upon me.

Do Good To Those Who Dispitefully Use You!

These words were surely not in my vocabulary.
They could only see my faults, but never theirs, and the Word of God calls this hypocritical (**Matthew 7:1-5 [AMP]**).

I heard voices from the dark side speaking to me, "Walk away and everything will be back to normal, everyone will be happy. You have disrupted the family. You are the problem." Some voices would say, "You talk too much."

It sometime seemed as though I was not able to get a handle on things, as misunderstandings suddenly arose all the more, and my head was bowed down in shame once again.

My ship had lost anchor, and I was drifting into the abyss. Silent cries could be heard from the depths of my soul, but only by me as the echoes would bounce back with a loud clinging sound.

I was looking to the arm of flesh for help in my turmoil, not realizing at the time that some would fail me. I just needed a listening ear!

But again, in some instances, I was the **captain** of my own ship. I opened my arms and welcomed persons who were not confidential into my personal life, having no wisdom in my selection or insight to know that I should have sought Godly counsel.

I made the decision to allow certain situations of my life to overwhelm me to such a degree that I was beginning to feel numb to the whole world, wondering what my purpose was.

Like electricity there were positive and negative connection coming from all directions.

I was hearing too many voices with instructions to do this and to do that. "You could do much better on your own."

I was not allowing the Holy Spirit to invade my spirit or to order my steps and direct my paths.

Psalm 119:133 (AMP) says,

"Establish my steps and direct them by [means of] your word; let not any iniquity have dominion over me."

So then I was drawn to the negative voices and to follow that path that seemed to be the easiest thing to do, as the process was taking far too long and I was becoming more frustrated and irritable.

Iniquity surely had rule over my soul. It had invaded my whole being. At the time the murmuring and complaining seemed like the easiest thing to do as I felt like Jehovah God was not hearing my prayers anyway. So I did not quote what the Word of God said about me and the situation.

(Joshua 1:8 AMP):

"This Book of the Law shall not depart out of your mouth, but you shall meditate on it day and night, that you may observe and do according to all that is written in it. For then you shall make your way prosperous, and than you shall deal wisely and have good success."

This was a cop-out. I felt like I was getting a release, though, from the venom that was about to be spewed out like an erupted volcano.

I was casting my cares upon others rather than upon the Lord.

There were many times when fellowshipping had become inconsequential, and I truly knew that the majority of the time, I was just going through the motions. I just wanted to be alone, away from everyone.

So I remained in a position where I just swam around in my "comfortable invisible bubble."

I felt what seemed to be like paralysis invading my muscles and limbs.

Fear gripped me to such an extent that I told no one of the experience and constantly thought of my family members, especially my children and grandchildren (and additional future ones), including great-grandchildren, and how I would want to live to a ripe old age and see them mature, get a good education, settle down with their own families, and contribute to their various societies.

Will my ship every find anchor? Will my soul ever again be anchored in the Lord Jesus Christ, the True Vine?

CHAPTER 2

Remembering

As I watch my grandson Lakoda, and granddaughter Kharis asleep, and then observe a smile now and then on their faces, I think that something pleasant must be going on with them. They look so peaceful, with not a care in the world, as all their needs are met by their parents and me presently.

I was in dire need to cuddle up to the **"Breasted One,"** my **"Heavenly Father,"** drink of His Word daily, and feel the love and comfort that only He could furnish.

I needed that spiritual sustenance so that my soul could be revived once again, be focused, and get back on the spiritual track.

Finally A Break

The periods of warmth that flooded my inner being felt soothing and relaxing.

Many nights I would lay awake, looking out of the windows at the sky, the moon, and stars some nights and others nights just listening to the beat of the rain.

My mind began to wander, inside my invisible bubble and in my moments of seclusion, and I began to roll back the curtain of time and recount past events and experiences, from my childhood and young adult years, with all the good and bad days, the dysfunction, hurts, pains, suffering, and so on.

I came from a family of sixteen siblings, namely, Albertha, Willamae, Creola, Michael (deceased), Frederick (deceased), myself, Dorothy, Emerald (my father's daughter), Vincent (deceased), Andrew, Kevin, Blaise, Peter, Keith, Bridgette, and Remilda.

In our home space was limited, but we had to make do in the situation and be content in the small four-room wooden house with the 'out-house' and the well that we had to get water for usage. I was always afraid of frogs that were lurking around in the well. We had to use a tin tub for our daily baths, making sure that the floor was dried from the spill afterwards. Eventually we moved in the larger house built of concrete, with the inside bathroom, that we helped build.

My mother experienced several miscarriages. I remembered when she was pregnant that there was no apparent morning sickness or other complaints, and nine months later there was the cry of another sister or brother.

My brother Keith has down syndrome and we all treasure him up to this very day, but more importantly he was my mother's pride and joy. He has been a participant in the special olympics games and has travelled extensivley, winning numerous awards and medals and has been on television, and even on the front cover of a well known international magazine many years ago.

My parents, Leviticus and Remilda Rolle, (both deceased) did their best to raise us with the funds that they accumulated through menial jobs and donations.

It was said that when I was born I was so tiny that they had to pin my clothes to a pillow in order to hold me, or to feel as though they indeed had a baby, as I resembled a tiny doll.

They often told me that it seemed as though I had every conceivable disease that was commonly known during those times.

There were frequent bouts of illnesses that I experienced, especially the whooping cough, as it was said that the sound of my cough was that of a loud, deep bark.

My puny body was invaded by parasites and covered with boils and sores. My mother made frequent visits to the health clinics with me, and the others, but also ensured the usage of Bahamian bush medicines that was steeped, boiled, or perhaps just the leaves were used, that killed the parasites and cured the boils and sores, such as Catnip, Cerasee, Bay Geranium, Aloe Vera, Gale of the Wind, Jack Mada, Croton, Five Fingers, Gum Elemi, Periwinkle, Sage, Lignum Vitae, Madeira Bark, Strong Back, Love Vine Cascarilla, White Elder, Mint, Pigeon-Plum, Shepherd's Needle, Salve Bush, leaves from the Breadfruit tree, Pound-Cake Bush, Red Pepper, Goat Pepper, and other bush Medicines, as well as Castor Oil, that were administered at certain times of the year or when necessary. She also kept a supply of Cod Liver Oil and Father John Cough Medicine to help boost our immune system.

My numerous infirmities resulted in my having received the last sacrament in the Catholic Church a few times, as they had given me up for dead. My mother said that they had already stretched my hands out beside me and watched as slime drained from the corners of my mouth. She said that my grandmother Lecita (deceased) once asked me who I was worrying about, and all I could do in my weak physical state, was to lift my puny hand and point to my mother.

I Shall Not Die But Live To Declare The Wonderous Works Of Jehovah God.

Time passed by, and this was thought to be nothing less than a miracle as I was closely monitored and remained a "sickly" girl up until my adolescent/early teenage years.

I grew to be very slim built and was called "bony shank" and "gaulin neck" by my siblings, especially by my brother Frederick. I have since learned how to appreciate my "long model neck" and appreciate the fact that I am fearfully and wonderfully made.

These names calling often made me very sad, and I began to feel and act, like an introvert.

I was very shy but did not realize at the time that this was not of God, and that He wanted to liberate me from such follies, not knowing then that I would be an ordained evangelist and years later an ordained pastor, preaching the Word of God without fear or intimidation.

The older children had to help with the younger ones as there were so many of us, and my mother had her hands full taking care of the entire needs of the household on a daily basis.

As children we played our part in the building of our second home just a few feet away, in that we had to tote rock and fill in the foundation. We watched as the house after a period of time was completed and was eager to move in.

I always asked my parents why they had built such a small home as the property afforded us room enough for a much larger one. But at that time there were insufficient funds to do so.

The house was nicely furnished and we were quite happy to join the ranks of others in the community who themselves had built modern homes with indoor plumbing and electricity.

There was the black-and-white television that I remember quite clearly that was turned off by my father early in the evenings. This was so we would save on electricity.

We had to go to bed early, cramped tight in the bed with other siblings, while the wooden windows were shut tight. We had to rise early to do the morning chores before going to school, and on weekends also before we had our recreation time.

It was a must that we go to church whenever the doors were opened and participate in as many activities as possible. This was also a time of fellowship and meeting our friends.

I always attained an excellent grade-point average and still am striving to maintain good spiritual and academic skills in everything that I do.

We ought to be a people of excellence striving daily to be the best that we can by the help of the Holy Spirit.

At age fourteen I thought I had a calling to be a nun. I always emulated them, the way in which they conducted themselves, their meditation, prayer life, and a life of seclusion. But even though plans were in the making for such a life, this never came to fruition as Jehovah God had other plans for me.

Of course I did not understand the spiritual aspect of this, the bad relationships that I would end up in, and the struggle in raising four children.

As an adult, looking back now, I realize that the Holy Spirit is bringing back to my remembrance the quiet times that I spent with Him and the revelation knowledge that was being imparted to me from a young age.

Continuing To Roll Back The Curtain

There were times when I would just wander off in the backyard and marvel at the fruit trees such as Avocado, Sugar Apple, Custard Apple, Soursap Breadfruit, Mango, Guinep, Papaya, Cherry, Sapodilla, Guava, Scarlet Plum, Hog Plum, Cocoa Plum, Seagrape, Goose Berry, Pomegranate, Tamarind, Coconut, Starprin, (that we used for chewing gum), Juju, and, and Pigeon-Plum, to name a few, and while in season delighting in them. We also got our natural daily vitamins from these sumptuous fruits.

There, too, was the variety of livestock that we raised for food such as pigs, chickens, and goats that as children we had to prepare for the meals. My father would set raccoon traps a little ways from home, and we had to go and watch the traps. But I detested the fact that I had to eat the meat of these livestock after having to watch them being slaughtered or told by my brother Frederick that it was slaughtered that day, just so he could have my share!

Of course there was the boil, fried or stewed fish, chicken souse, fried or stewed chicken along with the plain island grits that would sometime have dried conch and peas added to it, peas and rice, or plain white rice.

We had bags of grains such as Corn Meal that we cooked and added sweet milk to taste, Corn Grits, (yellow and white), and dried Conch that we also added to the rice or grits, Pigeon Peas (dried and green), Thyme, Onions and other food items that would come from the island of Exuma from my grandparents and other family members.

We found joy in planting and harvesting our own vegetables such as Cabbage, Tomatoes, Peas, Beans, Cassava, Beets, Sugar Cane, etc.

Then there were the usual pets such as dogs, cats, and of course rabbits that we all had to care for as well.

In the meantime we also had to collect food from the bushes away from home for the goats, and feed the pigs with bread, vegetables, or other leftover foods.

My greatest joy was collecting eggs from the chickens, especially the native ones, and filling the refrigerator with them. These were collected from the chicken coops or sometimes in the nearby bushes from those chickens that would periodically slip through the torn mesh wire.

I loved also to watch and handle the new chicks as they came forth so cute looking.

We delighted in watching our mother make the various breads such as raisin, coconut, sweet potato, cassava, white and whole wheat and also coconut tarts. There was a large oven in the backyard, and alongside it was kept a supply of fire coals ready to bake these delicious breads. I remember cutting banana leaves to cover those that needed it, as this was necessary for the breads to remain moist and also prevented burning.

It was so much fun to make peanut cakes, sesame seed or 'benny" cakes — which usually had a handful of peanuts — and of course coconut cakes. We had to grate and cut up the coconuts, and I hated doing this tedious job, as it left bruises on my fingers.

We had to be very careful not to let them burn, so there was constant stirring; afterwards there came the spreading out on the table, which formed them, and eating bits and pieces as we went along.

I remember the pancakes with bananas that from time to time I still delight in making, for my children and especially for my grandchildren Ambranette, A.J. and MeKel, who enjoys it with lots of butter and syrup. I dare not forget the Sapodilla pancakes with its extra sweet meat. These were both made with native eggs from our chickens, and were served with butter and sometimes syrup when it was available. Sometimes this was our only source of lunch with lemonade made fresh with the limes and lemons from our trees that we still call "switcha." We also used the leaves from trees "such as Avocado, Dill Seed, Shepherd's Needle and Fever Grass, with a little orange peel saved up and refrigerated from the oranges, that gave it an extra delightful flavor.

And of course I'm remembering the yummy soursap ice cream that we made ourselves on holidays or special occasions. It was a tiring task, and I did not like to participate in it, when we had to take the seeds out, then lots of sweet milk was added to the meat of the Soursap. The mixture was then placed in the ice cream maker and the lid tightly closed. The filled container was surrounded with ice and coarse salt. It was so delicious, and I am right now visualizing myself licking the centerpiece or the spoon.

On Becoming A Woman

All of us girls were sent to one of the monks when we reached a certain age for instructions into womanhood, which I detested.

My mother never hesitated to inflict physical punishments. I remember getting slapped upside the head or hit in the back when she heard the dishes clanging. She thought this was a sign that I did not want to wash them. I never cried, so she thought that I was always being very stubborn.

There were also the trips to the beach that we looked forward to in holiday times. The bags were prepared with delectable goodies, and we would walk to Montague Beach to enjoy the scenery, playing and wading in the water. Then it was evening time and the empty food containers, towels, and trash were gathered up. Afterwards we had our last dip to wash away the sand and started our journey home.

As I could recall, that was it for the beach until the next holiday.

I never learned how to swim, so I would sit at the edge of the water and allow the small rippling waves to overtake me as far as my waist, being careful not to let it go over my self-made boundary.

There were the other occasional outings for the older ones that we could not participate in. I must say here that I can visualize us younger ones crying behind the house or in the bedroom as we watch them ride off for their extra treats like a movie or a dance with our cousin and big brother Freddie Ramsey.

Peace And Joy
Laughter And Togetherness

Just thinking of it in my bubble gave me such warm feelings, feelings of togetherness, unity, peace, joy, and happiness that we experienced as a large family.

My mother taught us well, and this was the preparation stage for our adult lives and when we had our own families.

We were taught how to cook, clean, and iron.

I remember that whenever I cooked rice, it was always to soft or "saby" as we called it, and my mother would always fuss me for it.

The cleaning had to be done on a daily basis with the more difficult areas left for the weekend. We had to get on our knees and scrub the floors.

We didn't have the luxury of a washing machine either in those days, so we had to use tin tubs and wooden scrubbing board to wash our clothes. The whites were soaked in bleach for awhile to get rid of any stains, and this was under the watchful eyes of my mother, who ensured that everything we hung on the line was spotless, otherwise we would have to wash them all over again. We also had to iron our father's uniforms, ensuring that they were crisped and smooth; he worked at an airline for many eyars, cleaning the aircrafts and doing other chores.

Upon his return home we would search his bag for any goodies. We also chanced searching his pockets for coins when he came home stumbling from a bout of drinking after work, but the next morning when he was sobered up, he would ask for his money and we had to return every cent, unfortunately!

Stories were told to us by our mother of her washing the clothes for others and hanging them on the trees in back of the yard.

My mother also worked in an elite area of the island, as a maid, which benefited us, in that we were able to receive food, supplies, and clothing from her wealthy employers that she and daddy could not have afforded.

In our daily chores, I found it a pleasure to clean the colorful chicken-feed bags and wash them, and then my mother would cut them and make extra clothing for the girls. girls. We would starch them with cubes of starch, cooked until the mixture was firm, that kept them quite stiff, and then iron them, being so proud of additional pieces that were added to our wardrobe.

During my late teen years my family managed the cafeteria for awhile at an all-boys school that had classes from 8:00 a.m. until 8:00 p.m.

After school one of my daily chores would be to take the afternoon shift and serve in the cafeteria, selling hot dogs, hamburgers, drinks, cookies, candies, etc., something that I hated with a passion, being the shy individual that I was, resulting in my being taken advantage off by some of the students as they helped themselves to an occasional chocolate bar, cookie, or candy.

Whenever I would cross any of their paths, I would remind them that they still owed us some money for helping themselves to the various items. We would just laugh and embrace each other, as we reminisced for awhile on the good old safe days when children belong to the entire neighborhood or community and could be disciplined by anyone. Upon arriving home, when our parents heard about the misbehavior, we would then get a second chastening.

The nuns, monks, and priests took good care of the families in the community back then, getting our regular cheese and milk, so many bags per family that were distributed at certain times of the year. We all are so grateful to them.

How could I forget the "one shilling" coin to purchase a loaf of bread from Miss Ruth's shop! I remember my now-deceased brother Frederick getting quite upset in a loud manner, because he could only get one slice of the hot bread and butter.

It was a priviledge being under the tutelage of the nuns, especially Sis. Cecilia Albury, and others, who taught me well at St. Anselm's Catholic School, and then it was on to Aquinas College and the Technical Training College (night classes).

I rode to school on a bicycle, as there was no family car.

All through school I had very few friends and spent most of my time studying and burning the midnight oil. I studied secretarial science.

I involved myself also with singing in school and church choirs, as this is another of my passions.

My parents sacrificed for those of us who had higher education, and it surely paid off with me, and I will forever be grateful to them.

I remember the summer trips to Exuma and Eleuthera in the Bahamas and to Florida where we visited with my mother's brothers and their families and helped out in their restaurant.

I was truly happy, even though there were very few friends in my life, as I loved to be alone.

These were the innocent years when I was sheltered from the contamination or the negativism that was around me, as this was the preparation stage to do the work of the Lord.

I graduated at the top of the class at age seventeen and worked at various professions, such as in a hospital and for building contractors, engineers, quantity surveyors, the hotel industry, the legal profession, a general medical practitioner, and a nonprofit organization that deals with a certain type of physical illness.

Thoughts of my childhood came flooding in my mind and I felt happy at the memories of a large family with all its different personalities.

Sadness

But there were the moments of flashbacks in my invisible bubble of the various experiences I encountered that irritated my whole being, causing fear to grip my soul.

I am remembering my oldest brother Michael, who went missing many years ago, and was never found.

I am remembering my brother Vincent, who was stabbed to death almost thirty-five years ago.

And of course, I am remembering my deceased parents whose memories I will cherish forever.

The Days And Nights Of Loneliness!

As I grew older I became angry even at certain situations that I found myself in, which resulted in bitterness lodging in my heart.

Ephesians 4:26 (AMP):
"When angry, do not sin; do not ever let your wrath (your exasperation, your fury or indignation) last until the sun goes down."

The word *"bitter"* in this instance means:
- *exhibiting intense animosity*
- *harshly reproachful*
- *intensely unpleasant especially in coldness or rawness*
- *expressive of severe pain, grief, or regret*

One marriage and three children! These births were good ones — not too much sickness during the pregnancies and quite good deliveries.

My diligence paid off in the end, but looking back now I realize that I still could have achieved much more than I did if I had only pushed a little harder, but it's never too late to go after my dreams.

Even though my salary was very low, I still engaged in having housekeepers to help with Edrick, Heatherlyn, and DeMorbelle, and other times I was forced to place them in a nursery.

Very young and immature, I knew nothing about marriage, and that union ended in divorce after less than five years.

I foolishly entered into more unplanned relationships, and these experiences were so traumatic that they almost destroyed my physical and mental well-being.

Despite the fact that my self-esteem was very low, because of my loneliness I continued to search for love—but in all the wrong places.

I was very religious, going to church quite frequently and participating in just about all the events, but I had not given my life to the Lord Jesus Christ and made Him my Savior.

One of these relationships produced yet another child, Ambrozino. Throughout this pregnancy I experienced periods of hopelessness and thoughts of having a miscarriage.

This pregnancy was so unpleasant that my mother thought I would not live through it, but she did not tell me this until after the baby was born, a healthy 8 lb. 12 oz. boy.

That relationship only lasted for about two years and eight months, as I suffered yet more brokenness and disappointment.

Near-death Experiences

In my "invisible bubble," I agonized at the gruesome events that could have easily extinguished my existence.

The tragic events that were inflicted upon me physically, mentally and emotionally through no fault of mine periodically brought tears and bouts of fear to me.

The experience of a knife and a gun, on different occasions, being put to my head if not for the grace of Almighty God could have easily shattered my brain and wiped me out.

But glory to God, He had a plan for my life from before the foundation of the world as He allowed me to escape the hands of the enemy.

It was very difficult raising four children, as I had the responsibility of bringing them up as a single parent. Every aspect of their lives was in my hands.

We had occasional outings such as the movies, junkanoo, church bazaars, and Emancipation and Fox Hill Day celebrations that we all looked forward to.

Many weekends I feared going home, as upon arrival, on so many occasions, there was no electricity and no water (as we had an electric pump).

There was no form of entertainment and the children would then frequent the neighbors' to watch a little television or just go on the park to play basketball.

My mother would ensure that we had food to eat. Our weekly rations of various carefully cooked dishes and baked pastries were looked forward to, along with bags of miscellaneous groceries.

And then there were the dedicated friends like Conchita, Alqueena, and Elizabeth, who thought it not robbery to stop by occasionally with their contribution to our nearly bare cupboards. Sometimes they would also supply a fully prepared meal and also saw fit to give a financial donation for other necessities.

There were times when I was in need of transportation and compassionate friends and prayer partners, namely, Villadale, Conchita, Ruth, Marsha, Erma, Sheba, Deli, Maria, Barbara, Karen, Winifred, Olive, Etoy, Brenda, Elizabeth and Sylvia were available at times to assist me. Sometimes though I had to ride in a public bus when they were not available.

Some of these persons also, including my niece Mazette, occasionally supplied me a hot meal.

When I was in dire need of a computer, my cousin and godchild Jay, and cousins Raquel, Elmo, Aurelio, Alvarado and Sabrina were right there to give their assistance."

It seemed as though our favorite daily meal was corn flakes. My children and I when reminiscing would always talk about that, and some of them still have it today for breakfast.

When my oldest son, Edrick, graduated from college, our financial situation leveled off immediately, as he took on the role a financial advisor and leader ensuring that the house was not foreclosed, the utilities and other bills were paid, and the necessary food items were in the cupboards.

This role was played for many years, and still today his generosity towards us has not ceased.

The other children upon graduating had to make their contribution to the home as well. We decided who would pay what bill.

May the blessings of Almighty God continue to reign down upon them and their generations to come!

My form of discipline towards my four children became very rigid, and looking back I can conclude that these actions of mine were brought about because of the weights that I allowed to come upon me, and some that were thrust at me through no fault of mine.

I chose to remain in those abusive relationships for a much longer period of time than I should have.

I was heavily laden and frustrated and looked like a fish caught on a fishing line being hauled in to be killed, cleaned, and cooked. Yes, I thought that my hour had surely come.

Later on, through conversations with my children, I realized how I could have damaged them forever or perhaps even incarcerated for abuse, but I did not know at the time, as I was quite unaware of my actions.

My daughter Heatherlyn confronted me just before she left to go off to Missouri to do her doctorate in psychology and shared her experiences growing up in the home, and how she and I had only became friends at age seventeen.

She remembered the bad relationships and how I allowed myself to be used by these individuals that resulted in my negligence in sometimes properly caring for her, especially.

I was torn up over her recall and choked back tears, asking her to forgive me as I remembered very few of the details. She comforted me and said, "Mummy, you were searching for love. I was able to get healing from those hurts and neglect."

During the time of my writing this book, my four children my oldest Edrick, an accountant, banker, and portfolio manager and his wife Kimberley, an administrator and law student, and their daughters Kamerin and Kharis; my daughter Dr. Heatherlyn and her husband Dr. Louis, both psychologist and their firstborn, a son Lakoda Clarence Ekren, and is expecting again; my son DeMorbelle, who is active in the fine arts and also works as a beverage salesman, his children DeMeo, Aaron and MeKel; Ambrozino, a banker and mental health counselor and his wife Jennifer, an accountant who is presently studying for her C.P.A. degree, their children Ambranette, and A.J. are all doing well and continues to encourage and lavish their love on me whenever we meet or by our daily telephone conversations.

Yes, my children have seen me persevere through all the tough times and continues to pray for the Holy Spirit to bless me with strength and fortitude in the inner man, and good health on my life's journey so that I would be an asset to the Kingdom of God, my family and all those to whom I come in contact with.

What pleasure and joy it brings to my soul to see and hear my granddaughters Kamerin, and Ambranette both of whom are active in gymnastics and who enjoys reading, and MeKel, active in gymnastics and karate, and grandsons DeMeo and Aaron, both active in the fine arts and A.J. who loves sports especially basketball, pray for one another, and also for family members, friends and the children of the world.

Such strong, fervent, humble prayers of the pure and innocent! I give Almighty God thanks for their spiritual lives, and their various achievements both academically and in the fine arts.

Then to watch Lakoda and Kharis as I pray with and for them and also sing songs of thanksgiving, praise and worship to Jehovah God. They immediately cease whatever they are doing when they hear my voice, or gaze at my lips and my hand movements.

To God Be All The, Praise, Thanks, Honor And Glory For Where He Has Brought Us From

At intervals inside my bubble, there was so much warmth that embraced me at the very thought of my growing years.

During the occasional periods, I experienced moments of peace and tranquility and was able to dismiss the self-induced pain and the outside afflictions that had left so many inner scars.

I wished that I could remain in that comfortable environment of security but knew that sooner or later I had to face reality and deal with issues and decisions that were facing me on a daily basis that truly had me bound inside my invisible bubble.

Very few decisions had to be made by myself, as I awoke from the flashing scenes that brought me solace inside my bubble, because there was little to no stress that I was experiencing.

But it's reality check time again and I must face the music and finally deal with situations that had such a crippling effect on my mind, body, and soul.

I've Got To Go On, And I've Got To Go Through

CHAPTER 3

The Awakening

Comparable to a person coming out of a hypnotic state or waking up from surgery as the anesthetic begins to wear off, reality swiftly set in and I realized that I must make haste in my walk with the Lord.

Time Is Of The Essence.

I began to speak to myself, saying, "Why stay in this condition and die spiritually or physically or both? I must arise, brush myself off, and walk across the dividing line into my destiny, into my purpose."

My spirit, mostly through my own fault, was very lean and was in dire need of spiritual nurturing.

I Must Call On The Breasty One
I Must Return To My "First Love,"

The Lord Jesus Christ

There were so many times that I had to just say, **"Help me, Lord,"** as I could not even read or study the word effectively because I was not focused, I could not think straight.

Too much time was spent over the past ten and a half years in particular trying to find love or get others to love me. I did not realize that I was in spiritual adultery.

Psalm 55:4-8 (AMP):

"My heart is grievously pained within me, and the terrors of death have fallen upon me.

Fear and trembling have come upon me; horror and fright have overwhelmed me.

And I say, Oh, that I had wings like a dove! I would fly away and be at rest.

Yes, I would wander far away, I would lodge in the wilderness. Selah [pause, and calmly think of that!]

I would hasten to escape and to find a shelter from the stormy wind and tempest."

The stench of death continued to engulf me.

When I looked at myself in the mirror I saw my countenance fading and disappearing into a mist.

The fear also of just existing so many years and not fulfilling the purpose that Almighty God had predestined for my life frightened me!

Was my lifetime on this earth going to end in unfruitfulness?

Yes, the Lord had spoken to me many years ago and warned me of so many things through personal prophecies.

But He gives you a free will and would not force Himself on you. So I chose on many occasions not to heed to His Word, resulting in the long delay in my reaching a spiritual peak.

I was idolizing the situation and murmuring and complaining too much.

I asked myself so often, "What am I doing with the time that was entrusted to me?" And I gazed back and saw the many years that I had wasted when I could have done so many constructive things.

My God, Shall I Not Inherit Eternal Life?

This also placed great fears in me.

There were times when I experience great heaviness, and my body felt as though it weighed twice the amount.

There were panic and anxiety attacks, nervousness, and headaches, and bouts of fear also gripped my mind. I was spinning like a merry-go-round and had several close calls of falling to the ground.

My emotions were out of alignment, resulting in irrational decisions being made, but thank God for saving me — those decisions were never carried out.

I had to open up to a medical doctor and nurse, who warned me to take care of myself, as the level of stress could have very well crippled me or given me over to physical death.

(Well, spiritually I was drained.)

She said, he said, they said, but we did not say! This was surely not my identity.

CHAPTER 4

The Breakthrough

One day as a lay almost immobile, the phone rang. It was a dear friend, prayer partner and adopted sister, Bishop Erma F.E. Rahming Mackey, calling on behalf of herself and her husband, Bishop Raymond Mackey, both pastors at the time, to invite me to a prophetic conference that they were hosting at their church, "Wings of Faith Outreach Ministries International" in Behring Point, Andros Island, Bahamas.

I believe that this was a divine intervention in my life. I will forever be grateful to them.

Realization finally set in. For so long I had been slipping back and forth, in and out, thus preventing myself from obtaining the level in God that would allow me to walk and operate in His power.

Yes, this would be the turning point to get me from a babe stage in my life that I had retreated to and plunge me into the matured or manifested son stage (**1 Corinthians 3:1-3 AMP**).

I was leaving a place where all the noise in the market or the high waves of the ocean seemed to be insurmountable so much so that to a degree it felt as though my very life was being chocked out of me. My entire physical being ached severely, and for an extensive period of time I was unable to function to my full potential.

I Almost Let Go
I Was Right At The Edge Of A Breakthrough
But Couldn't See It
My Problems Had Me Bound
But Jesus Came And Found Me

The need arises for me to stop for a moment and say right here that as I am remembering this experience I am shedding some tears as I am so appreciative of the work of the Holy Spirit in my life during those four days and three nights of sessions.

I had to be taught the first principles all over again, in these closed, vigorous spiritual and mental sessions.

Repentance, forgiveness, then humility praying without ceasing for one another — in the home, in the neighborhood, in the community, the church, the government, the entire world.

Pray, Pray, Pray

I was prophesied to and taught how to walk in the wisdom of the Holy Spirit.

"The Kingdom Of God"

I was having a midnight experience like Paul and Silas. The chains that once had me bound were suddenly being loosed as I submitted my will to that of the Heavenly Father.

Not My Will But Yours Be Done

I almost let go, as the enemy had me bound, but God's grace and mercy kept me, so I didn't let go.

But when I think of His goodness and what He has done for me, when I think of His goodness and all that He has brought me through, all I can do is just give Him the praise.

I pondered at my state, and the time that I had wasted over the many years, and this was only because of disobedience to the Word of God, not submitting to His will.

Jesus, Jesus, Jesus Have Mercy On Me

Just like a wrestler, when his/her opponent thinks that they have won the match, and there is the trembling finger being lifted up to let the referee know that, hey, I am not out of the competition yet.

So out of the depths or the deep recesses of my soul, I began to arise and declare that ***I shall live and not die. I am fearfully and wonderfully made.***

I walked the streets, in the cool December month, looking over the waters and with hands lifted high to the heavens, gave Jehovah God continuous thanks for what He was doing in my life.

I begin to use my mouth to speak blessings over my life and over the lives of others.

I used Scriptures continuously to remind myself of the blessings that the Lord had promised me if I walked in obedience to His Word, studying and meditating daily so that I am built up in the inner man, rooted and grounded.

Decreeing, Declaring, Prophecying

Yes, the merging of my spirit, soul, and body had finally begun to take place.

Words that I had been hearing from the pulpit and through various media, such as radio and television, hounded me as I walked through the quiet streets of the island, "You are in need of inner healing. Cast those cares upon the Lord. Stay in the secret place. Stop rehearsing your past and all the negative experiences. Love yourself; take care of yourself. You need to go to God when there is a situation that would not change. Meditate on the Word of God daily. Cleanse your soul. Walk in the Spirit as this is where you get your victory."

On numerous occasions I have taught and preached the Word of God to others but allowed the stresses of life to overwhelm me causing the Word to be nullified or of no effect in my life to such a degree that I began to feel inadequate. This then is a sign of spiritual weakness.

I am getting older; why continue to bask in the pool of dark energy any longer?

The Word must now become alive in my situations and circumstances inside all my relationships.

I am reminded of my studies at Principles of Life Bible College where I was further taught the biblical principles for life's journey.

But I must now allow this information to become a practical everyday lifestyle.

Like the prodigal son in **Luke 15:11-32**, I had to return to my Heavenly Father, my Creator and the source of everything that I need to sustain me in this earthly life!

This Was A Life-or-death Situation

I must make haste and step back from *my* way of doing things, *my* rights, and apprehend Christ as the hour is getting late, when no man will be able to work.

I realized that so many things were not being done in divine order or in consultation with the Holy Spirit, resulting in much turmoil.

Matthew 6:33 (AMP):
"But seek (aim at and strive after) first of all, His" Kingdom and His righteousness (His way of doing and being right), and then all these things taken together will be given you besides."

Psalm 90:12 (AMP):
"So teach us to number our days, that we may get us a heart of wisdom."

Ecclesiastes 12:1-8 (AMP):
"Remember [earnestly] also your Creator [that you are not your own, but His property now] in the days of your youth, before the evil days come or the years draw near when you will say [of physical pleasures], I have no enjoyment in them—

Before the sun and the light and the moon and the stars are darkened [sight is impaired], and the clouds [of depression] return after the rain [of tears];

In the day when the keepers of the house [the hands and the arms] tremble, and the strong men [the feet and the knees] bow themselves, and the grinders [the molar teeth] cease because they are few, and those who look out of the windows [the eyes] are darkened;

When the doors [the lips] are shut in the streets and the sound of the grinding [of the teeth] is low, and one rises up at the voice of a bird and the crowing of a cock, and all the daughters of music [the voice and the ear] are brought low;

Also when [the old] are afraid of danger from that which is high, and fears are in the way, and the almond tree [their white hair] blooms, and the grasshopper [a little thing] is a burden, and desire and appetite fail, because man goes to his everlasting home and the mourners go about the streets or marketplaces.

[Remember your Creator earnestly now] before the silver cord [of life] is snapped apart, or the golden bowl is broken, or the pitcher is broken at the fountain, or the wheel broken at the cistern [and the whole circulatory system of the blood ceases to function];

Then shall the dust [out of which God made man's body] return to the earth as it was, and the spirit shall return to God Who gave it."

My mind began to wander in the midst of my bubble of the scripture verse.

Psalm 139:14 (KJV):

"I will praise thee; for I am fearfully and wonderfully made; marvelous are thy works; and that my soul knoweth right well."

Nehemiah 8:10 (AMP)

". . . And be not grieved and depressed, for the joy of the Lord is your strength and stronghold."

Gradually, deep down in the recesses of my soul, I could feel the Spirit of might rising on the inside. Scales began to drop from my spiritual eyes.

I must arise from my place of mental retardation and laxness and go forth and fulfill God's purpose for my life.

My spirit became hardened against the negative forces that surrounded me.

The **Book of Job** has inspired me in my daily walk after all the trouble and turmoil that he encountered, and in the last **chapters, 38 – 41,** the Lord spoke to **Job** and asked many questions.

He was also demanded some things of me, so I must gird up my loins, stand upright, and face reality.

I realized that I had to run for my life. I must be in hot pursuit of peace and harmony with myself and all mankind. I could no longer allow my lamp to go out.

Proverbs 4:23:
"Keep and guard your heart with all vigilance and above all that you guard, for out of it flow the springs of life."

Yes, I was beginning to finally see the light and realized that I must not remain in the state of stagnation any longer, but transformation must take place.

The Light Of Jehovah God Surrounds Me.

Submission to the Holy Spirit is always the first step, the key on which one's freedom hinges. So I allowed Him to do a circumcision in my soul, as I was depleted of spiritual strength and all I could do at this point in my life was to look up and cried to my Heavenly Father for help.

Isaiah 60:1 (AMP):

"Arise [from the depression and prostration in which circumstances have kept you—rise to a new life]! Shine (be radiant with the glory of the Lord], for your light has come, and the glory of the Lord has risen upon you!"

Psalm 121:1-8 (AMP):

"I will lift up my eyes to the hills [around Jerusalem, to sacred Mount Zion, and Mount Moriah]—From whence shall my help come?

My help comes from the Lord, Who made heaven and earth.

He will not allow your foot to slip or to be moved; He Who keeps you will not slumber.

Behold, He who keeps Israel will neither slumber nor sleep.

The Lord is your keeper; the Lord is your shade on your right hand [the side not carrying a shield].

The sun shall not smite you by day, nor the moon by night.

The Lord will keep you from all evil; He will keep your life.

The Lord will keep your going out and your coming in from this time forth and forevermore."

The **scriptures** came alive to me after all these years.

Philippians 4:13 (AMP):

"I have strength for all things in Christ Who empowers me [I am ready for anything and equal to anything through him Who infuses inner strength into me; I am self-sufficient in Christ's sufficiency]."

Proverbs 16:3 (AMP):

"Roll your works upon the Lord [commit and trust them wholly to Him; He will cause your thoughts to become agreeable to His will, and] so shall your plans be established and succeed."

My Creator would not leave me. He was with me from the beginning of time and will be with me until the end.

The inner man was beginning to get stronger and stronger. All the polluted spiritual attire was being shed layer by layer and the breakthrough from my invisible bubble was finally in view.

I Yield, I Yield

I saw myself soaring like an eagle. I was now looking down at the tribulations that I endured for many years and began to look at my present situation from God's perspective.

It seemed like the rough areas where decay had set in were now being transformed. My whole being seemed to suddenly be going through metamorphosis. Yes, a change was taking place deep within my soulish area.

Ezekiel 37:3 (AMP):
"And He said to me, Son of man, can these bones live? And I answered, O Lord God You know!"

My bones felt as though they had dried up, but its not over until God says so. I began to feel the Holy Spirit quickening my mortal body. The Potter was putting me back together again.

Philippians 1:6 (AMP):
"And I am convinced and sure of this very thing, that He Who began a good work in you will continue until the day of Jesus Christ [right up to the time of His return], developing [that good work] and perfecting and bringing it to full completion in you."

I began to stand back and detach myself from the situations that I had allowed to gain control over me, doing away with my will and whatever it was that was proving very arduous and allowing the Holy Spirit to work in my life as I apprehend Christ.

Don't Sell Yourself Short

I experienced in some relationships that persons may sometime try to get you to give over your will to them totally. Please remember that only the HOLY SPIRIT should be allowed to control your will. This then is control and intimidation, and is not godly or pleasing in the sight of Jehovah God.

Looking back at my situation reminds me of one of my favorite television program, *In The Womb*. This documentary illustrates the process of pregnancy, showing the baby from its conception to delivery, stage by stage, trimester by trimester.

I watched the millions of sperm as they raced toward the mother's womb to connect with the egg. The journey is a long and arduous one to the fallopian tubes. During the process most of them die, and only a few dozen finally reach the egg. The best one(s) are finally able to penetrate the fallopians.

I saw myself going through the processes of life as the sperm. The process can be very long and intricate, and at times you want to throw in the towel, but much nurturing must be done.

I'm reminded of my daughter Heatherlyn, who was almost eight months pregnant at the time of my starting to write this book with her and Louis' first child, my seventh grandchild and my fourth grandson (Lakoda Clarence Ekren Hoffman) and our daily conversations about the pregnancy.

There is much activity going on in the womb at this time, and the mother experiences much discomfort including vomiting, frequent urination, likes and dislikes for certain foods, nausea from the scent of certain perfumes, lotions, and household cleansers, irritability, and bouts of depression. She has even had a problem with the scent of freshly cut grass in her early trimester.

Throughout my four pregnancies there were three that went smoothly, but the fourth was one of much discomfort from start to finish.

So in my spiritual walk, going through the process of spiritual growth, there were weak moments when I allowed the flesh to overpower me.

I was not walking in the Spirit, resulting in many uncomfortable feelings and nauseated moments that almost chocked the very life out of me.

I found myself moving and stretching in my bubble. The cobwebs that encircled the pupil of my eyes were coming down.

God Knows Just How Much You Can Bear

Yes, I was sensing that a breakthrough was imminent.

I had also taken my focus of the Lord Jesus Christ and positioned it on the negative situations.

The invisible bubble was finally dissipating. It was beginning to vanish.

The spirit of heaviness was finally leaving.

To God Be All The Glory!

It resembled a person chewing bubble gum. A bubble is blown as big as it could go until eventually it stretches so much that it burst.

The process of elimination had begun to remove all negative elements, as the Lord has surely spoken to me inside my invisible bubble, and I must now do a spring cleaning.

I was willing to change and decided once and for all to do things the righteous way.

Proverbs 4:7 (AMP):

"**The beginning of Wisdom is: get Wisdom (skillful and godly Wisdom)! [For skillful and godly Wisdom is the principal thing.] And with all you have gotten, get understanding (discernment, comprehension, and interpretation).**"

I thought of judgment day and what I want to term "a hideous lifestyle": I said; he said; she said; they said; we said, all the works of the flesh, anger, resentment, bitterness, resulting in sleepless nights and physical ailments, and this put the reverential fear of the Lord again in me.

I Must See Him Face To Face!

Revelations 20:15 (AMP):

"**And if anyone's [name] was not found recorded in the Book of Life, he was hurled into the lake of fire.**"

I must get it together once and for all. Time is of the essence.

It all happened so suddenly. Yes, I sent up an SOS and was rescued by the power of the Holy Spirit!

CHAPTER 5

The Cleansing Process

I was not out the woods quite yet! Another journey was about to begin, and this would be a transition that was not completely new to me, as I had walked this journey many years ago when I was forced into a car, masked, and handcuffed with a gun pointed to my head and left for dead in a deserted area and found the next day.

My oldest son Edrick said that he had already prepared what he would say at my funeral service, but had to shake off the negative voices quickly.

In another instance, I had to run for my life as the gun was about to be pointed at my head, running through the neighborhood and searching for shelter from my abuser.

In yet another instance, I was held up at gunpoint and knifed, robbed, and physically taken advantage of. I took introspection of my life and began to appreciate who God had called me to be.

Vessel Of Honor, One Fit For The Master's Use. A Minister That Was Being Made.

I now had to begin the journey, which included acknowledgement, repentance, forgiveness, purification, and sanctification.

I realize that if restoration is to take place, I must allow the Holy Spirit to do a complete work in me. I must be restored back to my original state and walk in God's righteousness and holiness and His purpose and plan for my individual life.

It is a fact that I was a victim of physical, mental, emotional and verbal abuse through the various relationships.

I remember running for my life in the heavy rain and almost falling in the street which could have resulted in me losing my fourth child. I ended up behind a house in the neighborhood hiding until my brother came and rescued me.

I humbly asked Jehovah God to forgive me, and those whom I would have offended, and I also forgave myself. This alleviates the burden of you and places it on the Lord Jesus Christ so that the Holy Spirit could absorb it.

There is therefore repentance to Jehovah God, forgiveness to others and oneself, and turning away from the evil. Clemency is then bestowed upon you by Almighty God.

Jesus Christ Of Nazareth, Have Mercy On Me.

I realized that the baskets of hurts, wounds, bruises, and rejection I was toting around were just too many issues and it seemed as though I was in a boxing ring, but I had to release them all.

Even though I had escaped from my invisible bubble, now I must walk this walk circumspectly before my God and all those whom I come in contact with.

In one's daily Christian walk, the cleansing process is necessary so that there may be no blockage or hindrance in the work that the Lord has for you to do.

There must be no clogging up of your spiritual pipes, no residue, no stench of the works of the flesh.

You must now walk transparent before God and your fellowman.

I felt like a worm crawling on my knees. I humbled myself with silent crying out to Jehovah God as I forgave all the perpetrators who had invaded my life many years ago.

My heart was pliable, so the decision was made quickly to allow the Holy Spirit to cleanse me.

Again I had to come to a conscious decision that I could no longer allow the works of the flesh, especially gossip, anger, hatred, and the root of bitterness, to spring up in me. All the complaining and murmuring about the situation that I had found myself in had to cease.

I needed a sound mind to hear the voice of the Holy Spirit. I realized that spiritual wisdom is the key to successfully fulfilling the purpose to which I had been called.

Hebrews 4:12 (AMP):
"For the Word that God speaks is alive and full of power [making it active, operative, energizing, and effective]; it is sharper than any two-edged sword, penetrating to the dividing line of the breath of life (soul) and [the immortal] spirit, and of joints and marrow [of the deepest parts of our nature], exposing and sifting and analyzing and judging the very thoughts and purposes of the heart."

I went before God with all sincerity and humbled myself, as I did not want destruction to come my way.

You must allow the Holy Spirit to invade your whole being, going deep into the marrow of your bones, and remove all the particles and traces of sin or dead works that have been hindering your spiritual growth.

The only way, though, that this can be done is by totally surrendering ALL to the Holy Spirit. Read His instructions, His commandments, His precepts as set out in His Word, and be diligent in your study, so that you can be strengthened and edified.

Not My Will Lord Jesus, But Your Will Be Done.

I visualized tartar that is built up on the teeth. Just the thought of going to the dentist would sometimes bring fear. You want to have healthy clean teeth, and so after putting off the appointment you decide to give up and place yourself in his/her hands.

My dentist told me once that I am an excellent patient!

I realized though that the longer I waited to go in for a checkup the more the tartar would build up and the longer I would have to remain in the chair. She would not only clean but would search around the entire gum area and teeth looking carefully and paying attention to every little detail for cavities that would affect the entire tooth and other things that dentists look for. She would then proceed to carve out the defected areas, if not too far gone, clean and then fill them. Of course if too far gone the tooth would have to be removed and replaced.

Finally, you are satisfied with the end results and can once again feast on a variety of foods and drinks that were once hindered by the decayed tooth or teeth.

Explicit instructions are then given as to how to properly care for your teeth and gum. The dentist or dental hyienist would emphasize at the end of the visit the importance of adhering to these instructions and follow up visits. Finally, an appointment is then given for the next visit.

These instructions, which are so detailed, are important for the patient to follow for healthy teeth and gum.

So how much more we should allow the Holy Spirit to work on us just like we trust the dentist, or any other medical personnel for that matter, to care for our physical body and give us instructions. He is the only one capable of caring for our spirit man, if we allow Him to do so. The instructions for our life are found in the Word of God, which is the manual for spiritual life.

So again, I admonish you to not allow the works of the flesh to be found in your soul (Galatians 5:19-21).

If we allow the works of the flesh to continue to operate in our life, then we are operating or walking in iniquity, and the Lord will not hear our prayers.

We wonder why our prayers go unanswered and we are not getting anywhere in life. Check yourselves daily; perhaps the prayers are not like sweet-smelling incense into the nostril of Jehovah God.

Psalm 66:18 (AMP):

"If I regard iniquity in my heart, the Lord will not hear me;"

Unforgiveness can stand in your way to receiving the blessings of God. I have been experiencing the blessings of Jehovah Jireh in many various ways now.

The Holy Spirit will only work through a clean vessel and not if we are caught up in negative works that are fruitless to our spiritual growth.

Unforgiveness is heaviness or weights of the soul that keep one from progressing in the things of God and can be detrimental not only to one's spiritual life but to our physical bodies, and eventually destroy relationships.

After sincerely repenting and asking for forgiveness, I then experienced newness, and my body, soul, and spirit felt lightheartedness that I remembered experiencing when I got born again.

My mind is clearer to meditate on the things of God, resulting in my spiritual senses being developed to a higher level.

Scales have dropped from my spiritual eyes.

I Can See Clearly Now.
Glory Be To Jehovah God.

Hebrews 12:1-2 (AMP):
"Therefore then, since we are surrounded by so great a cloud of witnesses [who have borne testimony to the Truth], let us strip off and throw aside every encumbrance (unnecessary weight) and that sin which so readily (deftly and cleverly) clings to and entangles us, and let us run with patient endurance and steady and active persistence the appointed course of the race that is set before us.

Looking away [from all that will distract] to Jesus, Who is the Leader and the Source of our faith [giving the first incentive for our belief] and is also its Finisher bringing it to maturity and perfection]. He, for the joy [of obtaining the prize] that was set before Him, endured the cross, despising and ignoring the shame, and is now seated at the right hand of the throne of God."

You must also forgive yourself after you have asked God's forgiveness, setting your spirit free.

Hebrews 4:16 (AMP):
"Let us then fearlessly and confidently and boldly draw near to the throne of grace (the throne of God's unmerited favor to us sinners), that we may receive mercy [for our failures] and find grace to help in good time for every need [appropriate help and well-timed help, coming just when we need it]."

Let go and let God. Don't be chained anymore to your past mistakes. Forgive and distance yourself, but don't harbor the hate.

As you detach yourself from your negative attitude and mindset, and as the branch, purpose to remain attached to the Lord Jesus Christ, Who is the Vine, you will experience a transfusion of peace and tranquility like you've never experienced before.

Always ask yourself the question, "What did I contribute to this situation?"

I realized too, that the blessing of the Lord was not reigning down on me, as I had opened myself up to a curse.

Yes, I sometimes felt like my mouth was an open sepulcher, no control, running wild like an untamed mule.

There were some who tried to put the bit in my mouth but stubbornly I removed it.

The word *"sepulcher"* means:
- *tomb, grave, crypt, burial chamber, mausoleum, resting place, and vault.*

These are places where the dead are buried or placed.

The stench of death was swallowing me, and I began to feel as though I was being suffocated.

There was something awry about me. My spirit seemed to be moving around the earth realm aimlessly like a wandering soul who had lost all their faculties. Indeed this was not a pleasant feeling **(Psalm 94:17-19 [AMP])**.

Yes, I came to the realization that I must turn the negatives into positives, by turning from darkness and walking in the marvelous light of **the Lord Jesus Christ, the author and finisher of my faith.**

Time is of the essence. It is a precious commodity and rare like a precious stone.

In order for me to turn away from negativism I had to see myself being destroyed and loathed by others with a passion. I had to acknowledge that there was a struggle within my soul for freedom and a strong desire for peace of mind.

The Bible definition for the word *tongue* can be found in the book of James, chapter 3:5-10 (AMP), which says:

"Even so the tongue is a little member, and it can boast of great things. See how much wood or how great a forest a tiny spark can set ablaze!

And the tongue is a fire. [The tongue is a] world of wickedness set among our members, contaminating and depraving the whole body and setting on fire the wheel of birth (the cycle of man's nature), being itself ignited by hell (Gehenna).

For every kind of beast and bird, of reptile and sea animal, can be tamed and has been tamed by human genius (nature).

But the human tongue can be tamed by no man. It is a restless (undisciplined, irreconcilable) evil, full of deadly poison.

With it we bless the Lord and Father, and with it we curse men who were made in God's likeness!

Out of the same mouth come forth blessing and cursing. These things, my brethren, ought not to be so."

James 1:26 (AMP):

"If anyone thinks himself to be religious (piously observant of the external duties of his faith) and does not bridle his tongue but deludes his own heart, this person's religious service is worthless (futile, barren)."

Proverbs 18:20-21 (AMP):

"A man's [mortal] self shall be filled with the fruit of his mouth; and with the consequence of his words he must be satisfied [whether good of evil].

Death and life are in the power of the tongue, and they who indulge in it shall eat the fruit of it [for death or life]."

I was too free with my expression of words. In a lot of instances I was cursing and not blessing with my tongue, thereby bringing damnation to situations and circumstances inside of my relationships.

I myself set the course of my life by speaking negative words or allowing myself to be caught in negative conversations.

I watched a wheel as it turned around, and I am reminded that life is passing by, and that we have the free will to choose good or evil during those precious moments.

Ask yourself the question right now, "Did I unleash the gates of hell in my life?"

It is of the utmost importance to guard the gates or the openings to the soul: the eye gate, the nose gate, the ear gate, the feel gate, the mouth gate.

When going through the cleansing process one must not allow the works of the flesh to overwhelm or take control over us.

Take time to filter the programs that you watch on the television. Be aware of the conversations you listen to, as anything provocative or evil is damaging to the soul, as it will go into your conscious mind and settle in your subconsciousness to be recalled at anytime.

Watch your conversation; is it seasoned with grace? Is it edifying or is it pulling down and thereby bringing destruction to someone's character, whether it be family, friend, or another?

So why would you continue to allow the enemy to invade your soul? Don't you know that your body is the temple of the Holy Spirit and should not be used as an instrument of unrighteousness?

There is a saying that goes like this, "Be careful little eyes what you see, be careful little ear what you hear, be careful little mouth what you say, be careful little nose what you smell, and be careful flesh what you feel."

As you read this book, you must purpose to mortify the deeds of the body. Kill the flesh by detaching yourself from anything that would have you entangled in a negative web.

Imagine yourself in a washing machine or a dishwasher. Allow the Holy Spirit to wash away all the grit and grime from your soul. You're being scoured in all directions by the Word of God.

The Holy Spirit is cleansing all the filth that you allowed to contaminate your soul.

"There Is A Balm In Gilead To Heal The Sin Sick Soul, There Is A Balm In Gilead To Make The Wounded Whole."

Don't nurse your wounds, as this would only prolong the healing process. Allow the Holy Spirit to remove the bandage and pour into your wounds the heavenly healing balm.

Allow him to stroke and caress you, like a mother would carefully pamper her newborn baby, cuddling and holding him/her close to her breasts.

Allow yourself to feel the presence of a loving father with great big strong arms around you, saying, "My child, I love you."

People may have divulged your private business, causing your name to be scandalized, and added their five cents.

Get Over It!

Matthew 5:43-44 (AMP):
"You have heard that it was said, You shall love your neighbor and hate your enemy;
But I tell you, Love your enemies and pray for those who persecute you,"

I found out that my process for getting out of my invisible bubble was taking too long, as I was not listening to the still small voice of the Holy Spirit, but was walking in rebellion to the Word of God.

I began to talk out loud to myself so that my spirit would get the message.

I suddenly became increasingly diligent in my study of the Word of God, as I had been in prior years, knowing that my change would come.

A woman of God once told me, "Your change will come, not how I want it to or how you want it to, but it will come."

I prayed for the Holy Spirit to increase my faith. No, I don't want to go into another year carrying the weights of discouragement, emotional and mental stresses, but most importantly spiritual deficiencies.

I'm hearing clearer now more that I had been hearing for years. This was because I had allowed disappointment, anger, and bitterness to filter through my spiritual pipe, causing the blockage to occur.

Stop The Murmuring And The Complaining. Shut Up, Look Up, And Stay Prayed Up! Stop Allowing The Negative Records To Rewind Themselves In Your Mind.

Turn all these negatives into positives.

It's time to graduate from the baby stage of life and begin to eat strong meat, the meat of the Word."

You played a vital part in your drama by invitation to persons through conversation and sharing.

Matthew 12:34 (AMP):

"You offspring of vipers! How can you speak good things when you are evil (wicked)? For out of the fullness (the overflow, the superabundance) of the heart the mouth speaks."

Be controlled by the Holy Spirit only and never let anyone pull you into disclosure of personal affairs, whether it be yours or others. If this happens then it proves that you are weak, you have no spiritual strength and can easily be led by others.

Make a conscious decision to forgive and then release all past unforgiveness in your life so that the blessings of Jehovah God can reign down upon you, thereby fulfilling the purpose to which God has called you.

A mentor of mine once told me, "Those who don't have the capacity to forgive, don't have the capacity to love." Quite true!

Matthew 6:14-15 (AMP):

"For if you forgive people their trespasses [their reckless and willful sins, leaving them, letting them go, and giving up resentment], your heavenly Father will also forgive you.

But if you do not forgive others their trespasses [their reckless and willful sins, leaving them, letting them go,

and giving up resentment], neither will your Father forgive you your trespasses."

Again, let me reiterate that in all this I had to remember that I had a major part to play as *I was the initiator, writer, director, executive producer, editor, photographer, and set designer, and I played the lead role, and chose the others who were just the players or actors.*

Hebrews 12:14 (AMP):
"Strive to live in peace with everybody and pursue that consecration and holiness without which no one will [ever] see the Lord."

I care deeply for your souls and pray that you make a conscientious decision to shake yourself loose or disrobe yourself of the various defilements in your mortal body.

1 Corinthians 6:19-20 (AMP):
"Do you not know that your body is the temple (the very sanctuary) of the Holy Spirit Who lives within you, Whom you have received [as a Gift from God. You are not your own,

You were bought with a price [purchased preciousness and paid for, made His own]. So then, honor God and bring glory to Him in your body."

An excellent scripture to begin the cleansing process is **Psalm 51.**

Verse 10 (AMP) says,
"Create in me a clean heart, O God, and renew a right, preserving and steadfast spirit within me."

I had to get rid of all the weights that were causing me so much physical ailments and spiritual aridity (**Hebrews 12:11 (AMP):**You must first acknowledge that you have sinned, repent of the sin, and ask the Father for forgiveness.

Ask Him to purge you.

This word *"purge"* or *"purging"* means:
- *to clear of guilt; to free from moral or ceremonial*
- *defilement; to cause evacuation from (as the bowels); to make free of something unwanted.*

This reminds me of the old-fashioned way of cleaning out the system. When I was younger my mother would see to it that during a certain time of the year, we took castor oil and certain bush medicines for purging the worms or parasites out of the system. The taste was awful, but we dared not refuse to take it. She was only looking out for our well-being, for our health. We had to participate in this tradition, which was done on a yearly basis.

This process brings to mind the scripture in the book of **Hebrews 12:11 (AMP):**

"For the time being no discipline brings joy, but seems grievous and painful; but afterwards it yields a peaceable fruit of righteousness to those who have been trained by it [a harvest of fruit which consists in righteousness --in conformity to God's will in purpose, thought, and action, resulting in right living and right standing with God]."

So we must now also go through the process of purification.

The words *"purification"* or *"purify"* means:
- *To make pure; to clear from material defilement or imperfection; to free from guilt or moral or ceremonial blemish; to free from undesirable elements; to grow or become pure and clean.*

The word *"consecrate"* means:
- *dedicated to a sacred purpose; to devote to a purpose with or as if with deep solemnity or dedication.*

John 17:17 (AMP):
"Sanctify them [purify, consecrate, separate them for Yourself, make them holy] by Truth; Your Word is Truth."

Lastly, practice communing with the Heavenly Father each day. When you feel the urge to open your gates to negativity, the Holy Spirit will hastily bring an uncomfortable feeling to you. Purpose to always consult Him Who is your Standby, your Counselor. We must realize that every situation that we encounter as Christians inside our relationships we are being tested to see whether we will give the wrong, right or righteous response.

Perhaps you were late for a very important function like a family wedding, or a graduation that you did not attend, or whatever the case may be, and continue to beat yourself up, having sleepless nights because of the disappointment you caused to those family members or other persons concerned, and continue to say to yourself, I should have done this or that differently.

Apologize to all those concerned and ask them to forgive you. Move past the issue that was brought about because of your own carelessness, and allow the Holy Spirit to absorb the inner hurts and wounds. God is in the midst. It's all water under the bridge. Most assuredly, in the end Jehovah God will get the glory.

Learn from your past mistakes. Be on your guard in the future. Listen to that inner witness, the Holy Spirit, and be assured that He will give you wisdom as to how to handle situations or circumstances inside all of your relationships.

So many times we speak out of season or out of ignorance, not realizing the danger of opening up your soul concerning your personal business to individuals whom you thought to be spiritual. This is very dangerous, as there are many persons who would feed off your "drama" like vultures swarming around a dead carcass and who could care less about confidentiality.

The thing to do is to ask the Holy Spirit to put persons in your life that you could confide in. And of course starting right this very moment, refrain from being a blabbermouth.

There were times when I operated under the anointing of the Holy Spirit, but I knew exactly when this had stopped and also why.

Of course the Holy Spirit does not reside in a filthy temple and would not use such a person.

I realized that I was only going through the motions, as I had tried to smile but it was only pretense. Yes, the glory had departed.

In my invisible bubble, I knew exactly when the glory of God had departed from me, but it was now returning, evident as I began to feel the "Seven Flames of Fire" coming alive in me.

Isaiah 11:2 (AMP):
"And, the Spirit of the Lord shall rest upon Him — the Spirit of wisdom and understanding, the Spirit of counsel and might, the Spirit of knowledge and of the reverential and obedient fear of the Lord—"

In reality there would be a dark aura encircling you. Your light would have gone out. And yes, this would be visible to persons who are walking in the Spirit.

Ecclesiastes 10:1 (AMP):
"Dead flies caused the anointment of the perfumer to putrefy [and] send forth a vile odor; so does a little folly [in him who is valued for wisdom] outweigh wisdom and honor."

But if you harden your hearts toward to voice of the Holy Spirit, sowing unrighteous seeds, then you will reap a harvest of unrighteous seeds.

James 1:5 (AMP):

"If any of you is deficient in wisdom, let him ask of the giving God [Who gives] to everyone liberally and ungrudgingly, without reproaching or faultfinding, and it will be given him."

After all that I've been through I finally realized that my way of handling situations was not effective resulting in more chaos. I then yielded my spirit to the Holy Spirit for Him to do an inward circumcision.

Not My Will But Thy Will Be Done.

Proverbs 20:27 (AMP):

"The Spirit of man [that factor in human personality which proceeds immediately from God] is the lamp of the Lord, searching all his innermost parts."

The all-knowing God, who can hide from Him? He knows our very thoughts before we even think them. He knows our beginning to our ending.

So Let's Get Real And Take Off The Mask! He Is Our Creator.

It was at this point inside my invisible bubble that I finally acknowledged all the things that I was responsible for. I then decided that I must live a transparent life every day.

I owned up to my mistakes, repented, and asked forgiveness from Jehovah God and others as well.

I realized, too, that I was just wasting time and energy with mundane things and events when I could be exercising my gifts to be fruitful in the kingdom of God.

Garbage In — Garbage Out

I must also change my thinking patterns — from negative to positive. Also purpose daily to mortify the deeds of the body **(Colossians 3:5 [AMP]).**

The inner conflicts were in opposition to what Jehovah God had purposed for my life.

I want you to do a self check right now and see who you are giving access to your life or personal space.

Remember that you never know God until you know Him by yourself. So take the time every day to commune with the Holy Spirit.

Philippians 4:8 (AMP):
"For the rest, brethren, whatever is true, whatever is worthy of reverence and is honorable and seemly, whatever is just, whatever is pure, whatever is lovely and lovable, whatever is kind and winsome and gracious, if there is any virtue and excellence, if there is anything worthy of praise, think on and weigh and take account of these things [fix your minds on them]."

CHAPTER 6

Pressing on with Thanksgiving, Praise, and Worship

When I Think Of His Goodness
And What He's Done For Me,
When I Think Of His Goodness
And How He Set Me Free,
I Can't Stop From Giving Him
Thanks, Praise, And Worship

Psalm 32:7 (AMP):
"You are a hiding place for me; You, Lord, preserve me from trouble, You surround me with songs and shouts of deliverance. Selah [pause, and calmly of that]!"

Thanksgiving, praise, and worship unto Almighty God are the most important keys to coming out of the bubble of despair, hopelessness, and rejection, after having cleansed your soul of the filth, the grit, and the grime that had you contaminated.

The word *"thanksgiving"* means:
- *the act of giving thanks, a prayer expressing gratitude; a public acknowledgement or celebration of divine goodness*

The word *"praise"* means:
- *an expression of approval; admire; glorify; commend; extol; honor; eulogize; congratulate; pay tribute to; go into rapture over; applaud*

The word *"worship"* means:
- *reverence offered a divine being or supernatural power; an act of expressing such worship; extravagant respect, admiration for or devotion to an object of esteem*

There is so much power in thanksgiving, praise, and worship.

You praise and give Him thanks for what He has done for you.

You worship Him because of who He is — CREATOR OF ALL CREATIONS.

This is where an individual becomes more than a conqueror.

This is truly one's place of victory, prostrating before the King of Kings and Lord of Lords.

My countenance was different, and persons noticed that there was a glow on my face.

No more dark energy, but positive energy emanated from my being.

I flexed my spiritual muscles and began to awake early in the morning as I did before I allowed myself to be enclosed in a bubble, to give praises unto my God.

I would give Him thanks just for another day and to be able to breathe in the breath of life.

I felt my spirit man being strengthened, as I stepped back from the negative situations that I had no control over, staying in the secret place of the Most High (Psalm 91), and finally allowing Jehovah God to continually fight all my battles, but first making sure that my heart was pure towards all others, thereby walking in His righteousness.

I released all my burdens, cares, and concerns and cast them all on the Lord Jesus Christ.

I Can Do All Things Through Christ Who Strengthens Me.

I had a crucial moment where I needed to just touch and agree with someone in prayer, as the ground below me seemed to be swallowing me up, and not too long after that, the Holy Spirit sent two saints to pray with me at the point of my need, when my soul was sinking very low. He will also send the saints to pray with you.

Most importantly, after allowing the Holy Spirit to do a spiritual surgery in my soul, my mind suddenly became clear, and I would hear His voice giving me instructions.

A song would often come to my mind, saying, "**Go on my child, you will make it if you try**," the melodious, anointed voice of Bishop Erma F.E. Rahming Mackey.

As the various songs came to my mind, I began to sing praises and delighted myself in the Lord.

No, I Shall Not Die But Live To Declare The Goodness Of The Lord!

I committed those things that concerned me to Jehovah God.

Psalm 37:4-5 (AMP):

"Delight yourself also in the Lord, and He will give you the desires and secret partitions of your heart.

Commit your way to the Lord [roll and repose each care of your load on Him]; trust (lean on, rely on, and be confident) also in Him and He will bring it to pass."

Just to think of the creation of the universe would inspire you to open your mouth with praise and to fall on your face in worship of a mighty God.

Feel the wind sweep across your face, leaving a cool, heavenly sensation that leaves you with a deep appreciation for life and the Creator of all life. You can't see it, but you can feel the effects of it!

I marvel daily at the varieties of grains, fruits and flowers, with their majestic colors, shapes, sizes and fragrances! Only an awesome God could have created such things for us to have pleasure in.

Could you imagine that it was by His spoken words that the world was framed and that creation came into existence?

As I visited with my son Ambrozino, his children Ambranette and A.J., and his wife Jennifer, his fiancée at the time, and her parents, Dave and Vickie, sister Kattie and brother Matt, who was away to school at the time on February 2–8, 2007, in Illinois, during the conclusion of this book, I was in awe again of the beautiful snow that fell. Just to feel it against your skin is an experience that feels new every time. To see the trees all covered with white powdery substance, and all the rooftops and cars. How amazing!

A week later I visited my daughter Heatherlyn and her husband Louis in Colorado Springs, Colorado, while working on my manuscript, and experienced some sunny days and many days of snow and hail from February 8 to April 19. I had driven to the mountains on earlier visits, and seen them covered with snow and could only glance in awe at their beauty. This was my first experience though with hail and I decided to go outside to actually feel them as they dropped like marbles from the sky. I remember my son Ambrozino telling me of his first experience with hail in Illinois. He said he thought someone was shooting at him so he hurriedly dogged down in the car out of fear for his life.

What a mighty God we serve.

Other precious moments was the birth of their son, Lakoda Clarence Ekren Hoffman, on Friday, February 23, 2007, and the baby dedication that was witnessed by many, including the other grandparents, Clarence and Lynn Hoffman and my son Edrick and his wife Kimberley, who were godparents, their daughter, Kamerin. I would like to note here that Kimberley was pregnant at the time with Kharis.

I witness once again the awesomeness of the Creator and the revelation of how great and marvelous are the works of His hands.

When I looked at the species of dogs that they have, Amaha and Dante, I began to feel sorry for them as the snow came down. They just lay comfortably in the snow. I thought, "Oh God, You designed them to be just like that."

I can only think of the master behind all this, Jehovah God, Creator of the universe, and give Him thanks for His marvelous works.

Yes, all the glory belongs to Him, and He is to be honored and praise for His marvelous creation.

When I think of the goodness of the Lord towards me, yes readers, when I look back at what He has brought me through, my heart becomes glad with appreciation (**Psalm 116:1-19**).

Psalm 8:1-9 (AMP):

"O Lord, our Lord, how excellent (majestic and glorious) is Your name in all the earth! You have set Your glory on [or above] the heavens.

Out of the mouths of babes and unweaned infants. You have established strength because of Your foes, that You might silence the enemy and the avenger.

When I view and consider Your heavens, the work of Your fingers, the moon and the stars, which You have ordained and established,

What is man that You are mindful of him, and the son of [earthborn] man that You care for him?

Yet You have made him a little lower than God [or heavenly beings], and You have crowned him with glory and honor.

You made him to have dominion over the works of Your hands; You have put all things under his feet:

all sheep and oxen, yes, and the beasts of the field,

The birds of the air, and the fish of the sea, and whatever passes along the paths of the seas.

O Lord, our Lord, how excellent (majestic and glorious) is Your name in all the earth!"

Psalm 32:7 (AMP):

"You are a hiding place for me; You, Lord, preserve me from trouble, You surround me with songs and shouts of deliverance. Selah [pause, and calmly think of that]!"

As I began to worship Jehovah God, I sensed His peace that immediately enveloped me.

I surrendered my will to His perfect will.

I looked in the natural and saw that when kings and queens, princes and princesses, or other royalty enters a room, everyone would immediately stand at attention. Some would even bow in honor and respect.

When the national anthems of the various countries are played or sung, again everyone would immediately stand at attention, naturally giving honor where honor is due!

But, how much more should I recognize my Creator by giving Him all the honor and reverence due His holy name?

I think about the audible voice of God and when it was heard in biblical days by the prophets. Individuals would prostrate themselves in His presence. They truly acclaimed Him as Creator of Creations, and blessed His holy name.

Yes, He is to be worshipped, He is to be revered, as there is none like Him.

Right now, at this most sacred moment, don't allow any distractions to come to your mind. Remain focused. Center in on His supremacy, His incomparability. Draw from His well of salvation and be refreshed in your soul and spirit.

Think about the promises found in His Word and drink, as His well will never run dry.

You are now on holy ground, in His presence where no darkness can remain.

You are now in the Holy of Holies, beyond the Veil. Kneel before His Holy Throne, lifting holy hands. Prostrate yourself in the presence of your Creator, because He is altogether lovely, worthy, wonderful and holy.

Forget about everything; because He lives you can face tomorrow.

You are not forgotten; He knows your name.

So call on His holy name right now.

El Shadai
(The Almighty God)

Elohim
(The One True God)

El-elyon
(The Most High God)
Jehovah
(The Lord)

El Elohim
(The Lord God Of Gods)

Jehovah Tsidkenu
(The Lord My Righteousness)

Jehovah M'kaddesh
(The Lord Who Sanctifies)

Jehovah-Shalom
(The Lord Is Peace)

Jehovah Shama
(The Lord Is There)

Jehovah Rapha
(The God Your Healer)
Jehovah Jeireh
(The Lord My Provider)

Jehovah Nissi
(The Lord My Banner)

Jehovah Rohi
(The Lord My Shepherd)
Yahweh

He Is Creator Of All Creation
He Is King Of King
The Lord Of Lords
His Royal Highness
His Majesty
The Lily Of The Valley
The Bright And Morning Star
The Prince Of Peace
My Salvation
My Counsellor
My Shield And Buckler
My Mediator
My Redeemer
My Standby
My Waymaker

My Refuge And Strength
My Rock, My Fortress, And My Deliverer
My Comforter
My Hiding Place
My Help And Shield
My High Tower
My Strong Tower
My All In All
Holy, Holy, Holy
Is The Lord God Almighty,
The One Who Is And Is To Come
And So Much More . . .

Revelation 22:13 (AMP):
"I am the Alpha and the Omega, the First and the Last (the Before all and the End of all)."
I admonish you therefore, today, to:

Write A Thank-you Note
To Jehovah God Each Day

Start a journal **right now** and at the end of each day write those things that you are grateful that the Lord did for you.
You can start by just thanking Him for waking you up to see a brand new day!

CHAPTER 7

His Voice

The Holy Spirit is always speaking to us, but it's up to us as Christians to hear with spiritual ears, to take heed of what we have heard or read through the Word, and to walk in obedience to His voice.

He is daily giving us directions as to what to do, where to go, and whom to share with. But we allow the situations to sidetrack us.

The warning always comes before the exposure, and if one does not quickly REPENT and TURN AWAY FROM WHATEVER THE SIN IS, THEN EXPOSURE IS INEVITABLE OR **FORTHCOMING**.

2 Chronicles 7:14 (AMP):

"If My people, who are called by My name, shall humble themselves, pray, seek, crave, and require of necessity My face and turn from their wicked ways, then will I hear from heaven, forgive their sin, and heal their land."

Yes, I had a weak mind, knowing full well what **James in chapter 3** said about the *tongue*. Don't be like a mule, which is likened to a stubborn person. Allow the Holy Spirit to also be the bit in your mouth, guarding that unruly tongue. When He quickens you — **_TAKE HEED_** and **_ZIP IT UP!_**

You set up people as gods in your life, forgetting that He is a jealous God, and fall prey to the flesh, gratifying its earthly pull, which results at all times in spiritual death — separation from God.

Proverbs 3:5-8 (AMP):

"Lean on, trust in, and be confident in the Lord with all your heart and mind and do not rely on your own insight or understanding.

In all your ways know, recognize, and acknowledge Him, and He will direct and make straight and plain your paths.

Be not wise in your own eyes; reverently fear and worship the Lord and turn [entirely] away from evil.

It shall be health to your nerves and sinews, and marrow and moistening to your bones."

So often we allow the cares of the world to choke out the Word of God not being able to take root in our hearts; hence we experience fruitlessness or bareness in our spiritual life.

We fail to notice what Jehovah God is saying to us, as revelation knowledge is hidden because we read the Word of God, and it's only a scripture reading for the day.

Matthew 13:22 (AMP):

"As for what was sown among thorns, this is he who hears the Word, but the cares of the world and the pleasure and delight and glamour and deceitfulness of riches choke and suffocate the Word, and it yields no fruit."

Sometimes we allow situations and circumstances to cause us to divert and go into a slumbering state. In some instances we don't even realize what has happened until it is too late.

We're back in the muck and mire again dibbling and dabbling with the works of the flesh.

In my early Christian walk with the Lord, because my heart was pliable as I sincerely waited on the Lord, reading, and meditating on His Word, the Holy Spirit spoke to me, giving me audible instructions, and some of them I penned and kept like treasures. And in the process of writing this book the voice of the Holy Spirit echoed through my thoughts to share some of them with my readers.

So often, though, I fell from the instructions given to me by the Holy Spirit, but Jehovah God is faithful to His promise never to leave or forsake you.

Perhaps you too have heard the voice of the Lord speaking directly to you by the Holy Spirit, and I trust that this will bring you back on course as you begin to take note and listen with spiritual ears to what the Jehovah God is saying to you.

Keep a journal so that you could refer back to any personal prophecies given by the Holy Spirit when you feel as though you will yield or allow the flesh to overtake you.

It has taken me many years to really heed fully to the instructions of the Holy Spirit, in the inner solitude of my soul, but it's never too late to make a fresh start, a right about-turn and say, "I yield to you, Father."

Looking back now I have to thank God for the experience that I am now able to share with you so that you would not make the same mistakes that I did, or that you would recognize when the enemy is trying to destroy your character, or to cause strife inside relationships.

Make a conscious decision that today you want to make that change, regardless of your age.

As you give way to the Holy Spirit He will then lift you up. Allow Him to be the wind beneath your wings.

Don't allow situations or circumstances to cause you to abort what the Holy Spirit has spoken to your spirit.

Maybe the words that have been spoken to me can bear witness with your present walk with the Lord, and if you are hearing with spiritual ears what thus says the Lord to you the results will be glorious.

Again I Say To You Be Strong In The Lord And In The Power Of His Might.

HIS VOICE
MONDAY, JANUARY 22, 1999 (8:30 A.M.)

I have given each and every one of you a mind of your own; use it CONSTRUCTIVELY and not DESTRUCTIVELY.

If you have SCARS in your life, they can be turned into STARS.

Put your TRUST in Me, and do not LUST after the things of the world.

Do not MIND what people might say about you, because you can always FIND perfect peace with Me.

For you My people will SAVE the world through My power, as I GAVE you the assurance when I died on the cross.

You must always be on FIRE for Me, and never, never TIRE.

When you are going through a TRIAL period, just DIAL My number, which spells JESUS. I will always be waiting when you call.

QUENCH yourself in My Word, for you can be assured that I will DRENCH you from the crown of your head to the soles of your feet.

Always help those in NEED, for you will be doing a good DEED.

I want you to LIFT My Name up, for you will receive a blessed GIFT every time you do so.

You must be OBEDIENT to Me, and I will be EXPEDIENT in answering your needs.

WEDNESDAY, JUNE 1 1994 (1:30 p.m.)

My child, there are people complaining of pain in their body. I have given you a work to do — lay hands on the sick and they shall recover.

How can I accomplish My work through you if you do not act when I speak to you? Do not be embarrassed to lay hands on the sick in the name of My Son Jesus Christ — the Resurrected One.

You want to hold onto the keys of a building. I want to give you the keys to the kingdom of heaven. A building is only something temporal or physical — hold fast to that which is spiritual.

I have ordained you before the foundation of the world to do My will. Do not be ashamed to do My work. Walk in obedience to My will, but remember that My will must be done in your life — not what you want to do.

You must separate yourself from the world. Cleanse yourself through My Word daily. Do not let others hinder you with idle talk. My will must be done. Seek Me daily.

I have given you various responsibilities to do for a short time. I have even made the way clear that you can worship

Me without hindrances. Take advantage of the spare time I have given you. Redeem the time. Others will know that you have been spending it with Me.

Mortify your members and the deeds of the body. Your body is holy. Keep away from idle talk.

Commune with Me always! Do not get caught up in dead works.

You will travel, but you must get ready and prepare yourself now for that ministry. Spend quality time with Me.

My will must be done. Keep your focus on Me. Man can do you no harm.

Do not focus on the finances. You will be paid with eternal rewards. Do not murmur. Do not complain to others about the responsibilities I gave you to do. Do what needs to be done. I will deliver you. Cry out to Me. Why consult mere man? You have an open line of communication to Me. You are Mine. I will deliver you. Be joyful in all that you do until I sever the ties. Hold onto nothing of this world. These things will pass away. Do not fear man; You must fear Me who can destroy both body and soul. Look to Me, I say, for all that you desire.

Put your children and other family members in My hands. You cannot save them. Only I can do that. You will never be made ashamed.

Many will see My presence manifested through you. Look unto me from this day forward. Only to Me, your supplier of everything. Do not look to man. I will use My servants to speak to you, but you must keep your focus on Me. I created the heavens and the earth. I created man. I have chosen you. No man will hinder My work being done through you.

You must spend quality time with Me. There are too many distractions from the world. Yoke up to Me. Be wary of the counsel of man. You are in this world but not of this world. Learn how to listen for My voice. Stay in tune with Me.

Do not fear. I am always with you. You may feel as though I am far away, but know this, this day, that I have promised never to leave you or to forsake you.

Learn how to say, "I love you, Father," more often. Learn to say, "I am depending on You, Father, and not on flesh." You can do all things through Jesus Christ only.

Abide in Me always. Do not stray when in conversation with man. Look to no man. Yes, I have placed a fresh anointing on you this day, for I have much work for you to do. But you must not be afraid; I will strengthen you. You must always consult with My Holy Spirit. He will tell you what to say. You can do nothing on your own.

I have heard your many cries. I have seen your many tears. Know that I am bringing you into perfection but you must be tested and tried.

I am the Potter; you are the clay. Be directed only by My Holy Spirit. Abide in Me always.

Do not confer with man on anything. You are not alone. You serve a God who is faithful to His promises.

All is well. You are concerned about salvation for your household. Be not afraid for their protection, for I will protect your household. Do not take on the burden of trying to protect them. All is well. You must rely on Me. My ministering angels protect them daily.

Know this, My child, that all is well. Study My Word. Be faithful to My Word. My Word is life. Yes, there are many wells for you to drink from, and I will place them in your path and you will know that these wells are from Me.

Rest in Me, My child. Rely on Me. I created you and I know what you have need off. Look to Me. I am your Father and I love you.

<u>MONDAY, SEPTEMBER 4, 1994</u>

My child, because of your disobedience, I have had to chasten you in ways that may have seemed inhumane. You have to use so much water to flush out physical waste. Yes, you have asked for forgiveness in the past for sins committed, but allowed the very same things to seep back into your life again. I have had to bring you to a place of purging again, because of these very same sins (through outside influences). While at this location, for two weeks I did not allow anyone else to use these facilities. So is the stench of these facilities, so is the stench of your sins in my nostrils.

I am perfecting you, but you must go through daily purging. Then I will know that I can trust you to do My will for your life. Then I will know that you are clean, pure, and holy for My use only.

As I told you before, this present location is only a shadow of things. I use this to illustrate how I am making you into a minister, fit for My use only. But you must not get ahead of yourself. Be at peace.

Don't let outside influences hinder your spiritual growth.

Yes, My will shall be done in your life. I am teaching you. I am perfecting you. I am molding you into the character of My son, Jesus Christ. Your attitude must be mortified. Your mind must be renewed. Your whole being must come into subjection to My Holy Spirit.

Leave others to me. I will deal with them when I am ready. Don't hurry me with My work. You must let Me handle the situations. Just keep your focus on Me.

Pray more. Give Me more praise. Give Me more thanks. Desire to have a more intimate relationship with Me. Your focus is on things that are natural or physical. You must focus on the spiritual. When will you learn from mistakes? Walk always in the Spirit and you will not fulfill the lust of the flesh. Be joyous about the situations. Leave all to me. Do not even speak ill of anyone.

There is much work for you to do, but you hinder My work with complaints. I will deliver you very soon. Just rest in Me, though. Just rest in Me. Know that I am your Father. I have much to teach you. Be still and know that I am God. I will work great and mighty works through you, but you must remain clean, pure, and holy. There must be no blockage; otherwise I cannot use you.

Don't let those close to you who are not saved hinder you with idle talk; they are in need of salvation. Speak of Me to them much more than you have been doing.

Individuals can do you no harm. I am with you constantly. I promise that I will never leave you nor will I ever forsake you.

Yes, there is much more purging to be done. My Holy Spirit will bring to your attention those areas of your life that are in need of daily cleansing and purging.

Remain always in My Word. My Word is life. My Word is strength. My Word is filled with all the riches that you need to grow spiritually. Yes, My Word is food that you need every day to sustain you. I make provisions for the birds of the air, the fish of the sea, all the animals and cattle. Don't you think that I will provide for your every need? Are you so dull of hearing? When will you come to a place of total dependency on My Word? My timing is not like man's timing. Don't hurry My work.

The children of Israel have had to learn over and over again because of their disobedience and rebellion. They were a people who were stiff-necked. They could not wait as they were instructed, so they had to be taught the hard way over and over again.

Submit totally to Me. I created you. I know what you have need of in your human condition. Patience, My child. Have more patience. While My son was being persecuted for your sins He received this with much patience. He saw the end results. He knew His purpose — He had to redeem mankind back to Me. What do you think would have happened if He had decided not to go through His sufferings? Despite it all, He asked for forgiveness for those who persecuted Him. So it is with you.

You must forgive everyone and reconcile them back to Me. As My child, you have no reputation. Jesus Christ laid down His reputation for you. Yes, you must stay in position. I will tell you what next to do. I will send the help that you need, but have patience.

Trust Me alone. I will deliver you. Think it not strange when the fiery trials happen. Be very sure that you are anchored in the Rock, Jesus Christ. Hold fast to the Rock of your salvation. Do not try to break away from the Vine. Rest in Me. Your total sufficiency is in Me. There is much pain and suffering in doing My work. But you must remember that My Holy Spirit dwells within you. He will strengthen you to carry out the tasks that I have planned for you to do.

Be not too quick to speak to others regarding situations. Consult My Holy Spirit always. He will tell you what to say, but you must continue to walk in the Spirit. Listen for My voice. Be not dismayed. Stand still and see My salvation. Know that I will give you the resources necessary to fight your battles.

Warring angels stand ready to do battle on your behalf. I have seen your many tears, My child.

You have repented and I have forgiven you. Be still and know that I am the Lord God Almighty. I am a forgiving God. I am a compassionate God. I am merciful. Today, I pour out more grace upon you. I am the Lord your God. My Holy Spirit searches the reigns of the heart daily.

I have handpicked you from before the foundations of the world. Just remain faithful and keep your focus on Me. Yes, you are a human being, but remember that you are also a spirit being. So walk in the Spirit. You must stay hooked up to My Holy Spirit.

In everything, you must give Me thanks. Do not act like a rebellious child trying to get out of the grips of its father or mother while being chastened. Look at the end results — in the end you will yield a peaceable fruit of righteousness. My Holy Spirit is with you during your fiery trials. These trials are to make you more and more into the image of My son Jesus Christ.

Be still and know that all good and perfect gifts come from Me. Don't be moved by what you see in the natural. The hour is at hand for your deliverance. Yes, in My own time I will deal with those who oppress you. But you must learn from the oppression.

Soon, I will present you to the world. I will use you mightily to carry out My work. Be careful though, not to take any glory for My work. Others will be amazed at the way in which I will use you, but remember all that I do through you is to bring honor, praise, and glory to My name. Keep self out of the way. Die to self daily. Again I say, die to self daily. All glory belongs to Me alone. So be very careful when carrying out My tasks. Always make sure that self is out of the way. Always check your motives. There must never be any self gratitude or praise for My work. Please remember this, My child.

Rest in Me. Keep your focus on heavenly things always. Remember that My Holy Spirit is with you always.

I love you.

SATURDAY, APRIL 5, 1997 (2:00 a.m.)

I know of your desires. But desire more. I will take you to a higher level in Me. You will see this come to pass very shortly. Set your eyes on the work that I have called you to do.

I am a jealous God. I will reward you bountifully. Work faithfully. Work diligently. Be steadfast in your walk with Me. I will strengthen you in your hour of weakness.

I am all powerful and all knowing, and I have all your affairs in My hands. My servant Peter was not changed in a flash from a simple fisherman to a great leader and teacher, but through the very time of faithfulness — through the very time of denial, I was yet making him all that he should be.

Impetuous spokesman as he always was, ready to lead the other disciples. Peter could never have been the power he was had he not learned his weakness.

The Peter who was a mighty force for Me afterwards, who, more than all others, founded My church, was not even the Peter who said, "Thou art the son of the living God," but the Peter who denied Me, he who had trusted My forgiveness in his moment of abject remorse. He could best speak of Me as the Savior.

The kingdom of heaven can only be preached by those who have learned to prize the authority of the kingdom. A many-sided training My apostles need. Oh, joy. Oh, rejoice. I love you. Not one test too many would I lay on you.

SUNDAY, AUGUST 3, 1997 (6:30 a.m.)

My child, I will never leave you nor will I ever forsake you. There is no bond of union on earth to compare with the union between Me and a soul that loves Me. Priceless beyond earth's imaginings is that friendship. In the merging of heart and mind and will, a oneness results that only those who experience it can even dimly realize.

I love to pour My blessings down in rich choicest measure. But like the seed sowing, the ground must be prepared before the seed is dropped in. Your task is to prepare the soil — Mine is to drop the seed blessing into the prepared soil. Together we share in this, and joy in the harvest. Spend more time in soil preparing. Prayer fertilizes soil. There is much to do in preparation. This is a priceless time of initiation, but remember that the path of initiation is not for all, but only for those who have felt the sorrow-cup of the world that made a Savior and the tender plan of salvation who needs followers through whom He can accomplish His great work of salvation joyfully.

Glories and wonders are unfolding. Draw more and more into this wonderful eternal life. It is the flow of life eternal through spirit, mind, and body that cleanses, heals, restores, renews youth, and passes on from you to others, with the same miracle-working power.

Do not allow any circumstance or situation to paralyze you, stopping My miracle-working power from flowing through you. There is so much work for you to do. Allow Me to peel away the grave clothes that have been hindering your spiritual growth, caressing each layer as I perform this much-needed spiritual surgery. I need so much to wash away all the grey areas in your life. Yes, there is some pain — as with a band-aid being removed from an open wound of a child. Allow Me to do a complete uprooting of all hindrances in your life.

Learn to rest more in Me. If I, the Son of God, needed those times of quiet communion with My Father, alone, away from noise, from activity, then surely you need them too. Refilling with the Spirit is a need. That dwelling apart, that shutting yourself away in the secret place of your being away, alone with Me. From these times you come forth in power to bless and heal. My keeping power is never at fault, but only your realization of it. Not whether I can provide a shelter from the storm, but your failures to be sure of the security of that shelter.

Others may sometimes misunderstand how I am working through you, but do not focus of these misunderstandings. Do not allow yourself to be distracted. See yourself in a race, enduring to the end. Press on, My child. Past hurts, let them go; past disappointments, let them go; past experiences, let them go. Hold fast to that which is eternal. Look unto Me, the author and finisher of your faith. Cleanse your mind daily, filling yourself with Me.

Yes, I am taking you higher in Me than you have ever been before, but you must be ready. Don't allow anything or anyone to deplete your spiritual growth. Greater is He who is in you than He who is in the world. Seek My constant contact to know Me more and more. Make Me the one abiding presence of your day of which you are conscious all the time.

Seek to do less and to accomplish more, to achieve more. Doing is action — achievement is successful action. Remember that eternal life is the only lasting life, so that all that is done without being done in the power of My Spirit, My life, is passing. All done is that spirit-life undying. I will give unto them eternal life and they shall never perish; neither shall any pluck them out of My hands. So, eternal life means security too, safety.

Again, I say, detach yourself from anything that is not edifying you spiritually. I have all of your affairs in My hands — Your times are in My hands. Everything that so easily besets you must lay them on the altar of sacrifice today. Rest in Me. Do not get ahead of yourself.

Questions that have been stored in your mind will be answered one at a time. Wonders await you. Mysteries are unfolding gradually before your eyes. Joy in Me. I love you.

DATE NOT RECORDED

Even when you feel as though My presence is not there with you, I am present to bring deliverance and healing and to give you peace. I created you. I know everything about you. I am nearer than you think. Just a little while longer and I shall manifest Myself to you in a way in which you have never experienced. Continue to give Me praise. Continue to lift My name up. There no situation too hard for Me to rectify. You are Mine. I anoint you afresh today to do My will. You will fulfill the purpose to which you were called. You will speak My Word with boldness and clarity. Surrender totally to Me. Release all tension, all fears, and all anxieties. Continue to

Helen Patricia Rolle Rahming

seek Me diligently. Goodness and mercy shall always follow you. I will cause you to find favor with man. Do not be afraid. I have all your affairs in My hand.

CHAPTER 8

Conclusion

I am now walking in victory after victory, marching hand in hand with the Holy Spirit, and can honestly say the words of Martin Luther King, Jr.:

> *Free At Last, Free At Last,*
> *Thank God Almighty*
> *I'm Free At Last!*

All of the victories were not won overnight, as it was a process, and some took longer than others.

John 8:32 (AMP):
"And you will know the Truth, and the Truth will set you free."

The Truth Of The Matter

I acknowledge that I had complained and murmured too much, too often.

I acknowledge that my tongue caused hell's fire to manifest in my relationships both close and distant.

I acknowledge that for many years I did not forgive persons who had administered violent acts on me.

I acknowledge that I had a big problem forgiving those who verbally, sexually, emotionally and mentally abused me.

In all of the above acknowledgements, I had to come to grips with myself and,

Forgive, Forgive, Forgive.
Let Go And Let God.
Love, Love, Love.

It was then that things started leveling off and my inner man was finally at rest.

Hebrews 4:9-11 (AMP):

"**So then, there is still awaiting a full and complete Sabbath-rest reserved for the [true] people of God;**

For he who has once entered [God's] rest also has ceased from [the weariness and pain] of human labors, just as God rested from those labors peculiarly His own.

Let us therefore be zealous and exert ourselves and strive diligently to enter that rest [of God, to know and experience it for ourselves], that no one may fall or perish by the same kind of unbelief and disobedience [into which those in the wilderness fell]."

In my moments of despair, there had been numerous times when I felt despondent, but I encourage you today to always remember who God created you to be and have a determined mindset that you will fulfill the purpose for your life.

Surround yourself always with positive thinkers, those persons with godly wisdom that they can impart to you.

Detach from all negative environments or persons and from the mud slingers.

Too Much Talk

As with my life, there must come a time in your individual life when you come face to face with reality and are tired or fed up with all the **chitchat** and purpose to seek God's face for the answer. Your spirit man will get so weary of the murmuring and complaining.

Surrender all your cares and concerns to Him today.

My process took a very long route, as I was walking in disobedience to the Word of God. I did not **shut up** when He told me to.

Romans 8:28 (AMP):
"We are assured and know that [God being a partner in their labor] all things work together and are [fitting into a plan] for good to and for those who love God and are called according to [His] design and purpose."

Messages would come from the pulpit or a word from a television program that will warn you to get back on track and prompt you to direct your energies to reading and meditating on His Word daily.

Other times you will be reminded through simple things such as looking at His marvelous creation and realizing that you are not even appreciative of His handiworks.

Don't Be Dull Of Hearing, Take Heed How You Hear.

As your read my biography, perhaps you are saying, "That sounds like my story. I went through some of the same issues. Yes, the Lord has been speaking to me in personal prophecies."

Go after God with all that you've got — your whole being. Your life depends on it.

Allow the Holy Spirit to chisel out all negative roots when they spring up and stretch Himself out in you.

Psalm 42:7 (AMP):

"[Roaring] deep calls to [roaring] deep at the thunder of Your waterspouts; all Your breakers and Your rolling waves have gone over me."

The Holy Spirit will send persons into your life to help you get back on your course or path to destiny.

He used my biological children to be a source of encouragement to me on a frequent basis when I felt like giving up or retaliating, saying to me that "all was not lost; this too shall pass; things will get better."

They would always say, "Don't worry. God is going to see you through all your troubles and worries. Just hold on. One day you will rise above the shame and God will reward and give you an abundance that you deserve. You will be self-sufficient. Remember that we are all here for you. God has brought the five of us from a long way. Don't let go; we love you."

In their words of encouragement we would talk about the experiences that we went through and thank Almighty God for where we are today.

Just the words *"I love you,"* give me a booster shot in the deep recesses of my soul every time.

Numerous friends had a part to play as well, as they would call or meet me and say words of encouragement, reassuring me that they loved me and that they were praying continuously for me.

These constant words would resound in my ear, shaking my inner being, infusing strength back into the marrow of my bones, the nourishment that I needed on a daily basis to rise up.

But who can love me more than any human being can?

John 3:16 (AMP):

"For God so greatly loved and dearly prized the world that He [even] gave up His only begotten (unique) Son, so that whoever believes in (trusts in, clings to, relies on) Him shall not perish (come to destruction, be lost) but have eternal (everlasting) life."

I find it soothing when reading the Word, to see how the writers expressed themselves and made Him so BIG in their lives.

The book of **Romans** for salvation and general principles for Christian living, **Psalms** for thanksgiving praise and worship, **Proverbs** as a tool for skillful and godly wisdom, are excellent books for those who have never really studied the Word of God in-depth.

Like a woman in childbirth, push through that thick layer of flesh-like bubble until you experience that newness, that refreshing feeling like the air in spring time.

Yes, go to the next level that the Lord has for you.

God Is Constant; He Never Changes.

Pour out yourself before Him even though He knows all about you. Ask Him to increase your faith.

I believe that on my life's journey I was interrupted for a purpose - for me to walk in the glory of God and the power of His Holy Spirit with all the spiritual, physical and material blessings as well poured on my life in a greater demension.

Stay in His presence. Meditate daily on His Word, and ask for revelation knowledge from the Holy Spirit.

Allow the Holy Spirit to flush out every fear. Don't let negative thoughts stay in your mind.

Let your inner man be framed by the Word of God.

Psalm 119:105 (AMP):

"Your word is a lamp to my feet and a light to my path."

Reflect on the most precious commodity, *"time"* that Jehovah God has given to us all.

Start a clean slate today. Do away with the old and allow the new to envelope your life today.

It's never too late, and you're never too old in age to ask the Lord to fix or mend all your broken pieces back together again.

You should never be too frightened to put things on the sidewalk that don't serve you any longer for the Holy Spirit to absorb, and make way for the new.

Perhaps there are persons that you are thinking about right this very moment whom you need to detach yourself from. Ask the Holy Spirit for the wisdom to do so, as neglecting this move will eventually stifle your spiritual growth and cause the gates of hell to pour out its wrath upon you.

Welcome the abundance of the kingdom of heaven in all your affairs, as all that is good and perfect comes from the Heavenly Father.

Make a firm decision that you will walk in the fruit of the Holy Spirit.

Galatians 5:22-24 (AMP):

"But the fruit of the [Holy] Spirit [the work which His presence within accomplishes] is love, joy (gladness),

peace, patience (an even temper, forbearance), kindness, goodness (benevolence), faithfulness,

Gentleness, (meekness, humility), self-control (self-restraint, continence). Against such things there is no law *[that can bring a charge]."*

Shake Off Those Heavy Bands That Encircle Your Mind.

Isaiah 60:1 (AMP):
"Arise [from the depression and prostration in which circumstances have kept you—rise to a new life]! Shine (be radiant with the glory of the Lord), for your light has come, and the glory of the Lord has risen upon you!"

Purpose to live in the light and never the dark, as no darkness can penetrate light, but light will always dispel darkness.

The flesh is continuously warring against the Spirit. My advice to you then is to look up all scriptures dealing with the flesh. Study them. Memorize them. Write them down on flash cards and place them in significant areas of your home and even in your wallets or purses.

Hebrews 12:14 (AMP) says,
"Strive to live in peace with everybody and pursue that consecration and holiness without which no one will [ever] see the Lord."

In the book of **Genesis in chapter 18,** God told Abraham that his wife Sarah would bear a son. Sarah laughed to herself because she was of her age (past childbearing age), but the Lord said in **verse 14,**

"Is there anything too hard or too wonderful for the Lord?"

As I have done, I now admonish you to rise and be all that Jehovah God has created you to be.

Away with **mediocrity** or being **mediocre, meaning:**
- *of moderate or low quality, value, ability, or performance*

This type of life is the lower life and not the higher.

Apprehend **excellence**, meaning:
- *an excellent or valuable quality.*

The word ***"excel"*** means:
- *to rise, project; to be superior to; surpass in accomplishment or achievement;*
- *to be distinguishable by superiority; surpass others.*

This is the higher life, the life found in Christ Jesus.

Now these words sound like adjectives describing one of royalty, and we are a "royal priesthood."

As I look at the word ***"royal"*** it means:
- *of kingly ancestry.*

We've got the blood of the Lord Jesus Christ running through our veins; we were regenerated when we got saved.

So, then, as believers, we are royal priests and must purpose never again to allow the enemy to cheat us of our inheritance, which can only result in our living a low-down dirty life, which is not pleasing in the sight of Almighty God.

We were created to be the best at everything we do.

You Are Fearfully And Wonderfully Made!

Our fingerprints, footprints, and teeth are the originals and there are no copies or duplicates anywhere in the universe. The mold has been broken. Remember that you are uniquely custom made for God's purpose. You are not a mistake.

I admonish you to not let sin of any nature continue to have dominion or rule over you.

It is important to your spiritual growth that you also release all past hurts and wounds and allow the Holy Spirit to seal you with His love.

Sure we make mistakes that cause us to be encapsulated in a bubble-like environment, regretting that we ever put ourselves in those unfortunate situations. But, guess what, it's time to **"let go"** of all that stuff and **"let God"** do a work in your life.

I am a witness. I can testify. Yes, I am a living testimony that holding on will destroy you completely — body, soul, and spirit.

So don't you want to reap the eternal rewards that Jehovah God has for you?

Revelation 22:12-14 (AMP):

"Behold, I am coming soon, and I shall bring My wages and rewards with Me, to repay and render to each one just what his own actions and his own work merit.

I am the Alpha and the Omega, the First and the Last (the Before all and the End of all).

Blessed (happy and to be envied) are those who cleanse their garments, that they may have the authority and right to [approach] the tree of life and to enter through the gates into the city."

Psalm 24:3-5 (AMP):

"Who shall go up into the mountain of the Lord? Or who shall stand in His Holy Place?

He who has clean hands and a pure heart, who has not lifted himself up to falsehood or to what is false, nor sworn deceitfully.

He shall receive blessing from the Lord and righteousness from the God of his salvation."

I speak to your spirit man this very moment and command you in the name of the Lord Jesus Christ of Nazareth to:

Let Go And Let God!

Hold your heads high, stick your chest out, and see yourself being all that Jehovah God has ordained you to be.

Those persons who **depreciated** you will soon learn how to **appreciate** you.

When you are weak then you are made strong through the blood of Jesus Christ.

Put your hands in the hands of the Man who calmed the seas, parted the red sea, healed the blind, opened deaf ears, and caused the lame to walk.

And keep your hands in the hands of the Man who became the **sacrificial lamb** for the world.

The arm of flesh will surely fail you, as it is imperfect and will return to the dust from whence it was made.

Let your hope be in the Creator of Creations today. His grace is sufficient for all your needs.

My Hope Is Built On Nothing Less,
Than Jesus' Blood And Righteousness,
I Dare Not Trust The Sweetest Frame,
But Wholly Lean On Jesus' Name,
On Christ The Solid Rock I Stand,
All Other Ground Is Sinking Sand,
All Other Ground Is Sinking Sand.

Know, This Day, That Your Life Is Hid In Christ Jesus.

I look at a "love vine," grown in this region, the islands of the Caribbean, and notice it carefully whenever I pass by one, the way in which each vine is entangled around one another.

I have handled this vine in my early years and I know that it is a tough vine to loosen.

It continues to remind me of how much more I must **remain hooked up to the Lord Jesus Christ, the True Vine (John 15:1-27), and wrapped up in His Word daily, as He is the Bread of Life (John 6:35).** The rough winds began to roar, the trees began to sway, there was a loud crash, and I saw that an avocado tree in our yard had fallen under the fierceness of the strong winds.

I looked at the trunk of the tree and saw that it had been broken, but not completely severed, thus allowing the leaves to remain green and the fruits that were left to get riper.

This was the result of the connection. The tree was still getting its nourishment from the soil; therefore the fruits continued to be fed the necessary ingredients to grow to their full potential. And a few months later, the branches have gotten firm once again and ready to grow into maturity, yielding more avocado.

Well, sometimes we feel as though we are completely cut off from the Holy Spirit, but there is a ray or glimmer of hope beyond the dark shadows. Just purpose that you would focus on that area, and eventually you will be empowered and once again walk in your full potential.

There was a point in my life where I felt powerless, as though the "anointing had left my life." I seem to be void of the flow from my spiritual connection, the Holy Spirit, and felt cut off from the Vine.

I was still praying for others but felt as though nothing would happen. As I mentioned before, I was just going through the motions!

Can You Identify With This?

I had to come to the realization also that my identity was not in individuals but in my Creator.

Yes, only the manufacturer could put me back together again; every piece of my soul that I had given away negatively through all my relationships, from the east, west, north and south. I needed to be made whole once again.

James 4:10 (AMP):

"Humble yourselves [feeling very insignificant] in the presence of the Lord, and He will exalt you [He will lift you up and make your lives significant]."

It's time now to allow the process of change to begin, like a caterpillar into a beautiful butterfly. It always amazes me to observe how, in this instant, metamorphosis or transformation takes place. Nothing is impossible for Him to do. El Shadai — the Almighty God.

Again, look at your present state and purpose to pray for others, that their road to victory may begin as soon as possible.

It does not mean that your trials have ceased as sometimes it would seem as though you are going under again, but know that God is with you and He will never leave or forsake you.

Right now, inside of your relationship, you may be experiencing rejection from a spouse, emotional and mental abuse, but hold on, remain focused, walk in love and be sweet. Seek the Holy Spirit for wisdom as to what to do in this instance. You may be going through physical abuse, which may warrant departure for your safety. It is incumbent upon you to seek the voice of the Holy Spirit and be assured that He will give you wisdom as to how to handle your particular situation which will lead you to your pathway to victory.

It's Only A Matter Of Time Before Your Breakthrough.
I'm remembering in the Book of Acts where Paul and Silas were thrown in jail.
Acts 16:25-26 (AMP):
"But about midnight, as Paul and Silas were praying and singing hymns of praise to God, and the [other] prisoners were listening to them,
Suddenly there was a great earthquake, so that the very foundations of the prison were shaken; and at once all the doors were opened and everyone's shackles were unfastened."
Psalm 34:17 (AMP):
"When the righteous cry for help, the Lord hears, and delivers them out of all their distress and troubles."

Stop Wavering, Take Your Position, And Stand Firm On The Word Of God.

*Stop Focusing On The Negative
And Focus On The Positive.
Stop The Victim Mentally And Feeling
Remorseful For Yourself.*

Allow The Holy Spirit To Harness All Those Negative Emotions.
You Are Fearfully and Wonderfully Made.

As you read my experiences:

I pray that Jehovah Rapha, the God that healeth, would heal you from all past hurts, inner wounds, and disappointments.

I pray that Jehovah-Shalom, the Lord of peace, would bestow upon you His peace.

I pray that you would experience, as I am now experiencing, the fresh wind of the Holy Spirit, and that your spirit, soul, and body would merge.

I pray that your route to victory is shortened as you submit fully to the leading of the Holy Spirit, allowing Him to keep your feet from falling into unrighteousness.

I pray that you would not digress into the pit of regrets, or into the slum of degradation, but move from the realm of mediocrity and darkness into the arena of excellence, God's marvelous light.

I pray that you would appreciate El Shadai, the Almighty God, for the things that He has done for you — the situations that He has brought you out of as you made your bed in the enemies' camp.

He might have delivered you from works of the flesh that can result in spiritual and sometimes even physical death, such as **gossip, adultery, fornication, lying, prostitution, pride, greed, manipulation, stealing, jealousy, envy, unforgiveness, drug addiction, etc.**

So I pray that you faint not, but gird up the loins of your mind through the Word of God.

Galatians 6:9 (AMP):
"And let us not lose heart and grow weary and faint in acting nobly and doing right, for in due time and at the appointed season we shall reap, if we do not loosen and relax our courage and faint."

Start a journal and every day write down your experiences that you have encountered and thank God for them, such as a sound mind and a healthy body.

Philippians 4:9 (AMP):
"Practice what you have learned and received and heard and seen in me, and model your way of living on it, and the God of peace (of untroubled, undisturbed well-being) will be with you."

I have gained much wisdom from my experiences, and have learnt how to be discreet and selective in my relationships.

I have learned so many great lessons during my remembering stage of my invisible bubble, about genuine and false relationships. Those who have your back and those who will stab you in the back. Conflicts will arise from time to time, but it's up to you, as an individual who has cleansed yourselves from the filthiness of the flesh, to purpose to live an exemplary life before Jehovah God and mankind.

Remember too that everything that you have ever encountered in your life God allowed to happen for a purpose. So you must see God in every situation, in all circumstances inside of all your relationships.

Yes, you are being tested to see what your response would be.

When condition in a relationship does not change then I believe that the Lord will take your hand and lead you out. But you must humble yourself, and this will set you up for what is due to you.

I was tired of unforgiveness and the murmuring and complaining, and I knew for sure that I had to **Let go and Let God.**

The wilderness experiences were becoming so mundane to me.

I had to purpose that TODAY I will manifest the Glory of God.

Purpose right now as you read this book that you will cast all your cares on the **"Burden Bearer."**

Psalm 101:2 (AMP):

"I will behave myself wisely and give heed to the blameless way—O when will You come to me? I will walk within my house in integrity and with a blameless heart."

Proverbs 15:1 (AMP):

"A soft answer turns away wrath, but grievous words stir up anger."

In everything we do we need the wisdom of God in order for it to be successful, whether it be how to manage a relationship, completing a project, seeking a career or whatever the case may be.

Proverbs 8:35 (AMP):

"For whoever finds me [Wisdom] finds life and draws forth and obtains favor from the Lord."

In summation I would like to say that after the cleansing process I am experiencing the peace of God that surpasses all human understanding.

I am now following the leading of the Holy Spirit. I sincerely believe that I have been reinstated in the army of the Lord Jesus Christ and am ready to do His bidding.

ISAIAH 41:10-13 (AMP):

"Fear not [there is nothing to fear], for I am with you; do not look around you in terror and be dismayed, for I am your God. I will strengthen and harden you to difficulties, yes, I will help you; yes I will hold you up and with My [victorious] right hand of rightness and justice.

Behold, all they who are enraged and inflamed against you shall be put to shame and confounded; they who strive against you shall be as nothing and shall perish.

You shall seek those who contend with you but shall not find them; they who war against you shall be as nothing, as nothing at all.

For I the Lord your God hold your right hand; I am the Lord, Who says to you, Fear not; I will help you!"

Running Back To My First Love

I can now say, "Lord I am available; use me for your honor and glory."

Jesus Is With Us In Times We Mourn,
Has Never Left Is Since We Were Born,
With Loving Arms He Comforts The Soul,
And Put Our Lives Back In Control.

Jeremiah 29:11-13 (AMP):
"For I know the thoughts and plans that I have for you, says the Lord, thoughts and plans for welfare and peace and not for evil, to give you hope in your final outcome.

Then you will call upon Me, and you will come and pray to Me, and I will hear and heed you.

Then you will seek Me, inquire for, and require Me [as a vital necessity] and find Me when you search for Me with all your heart."

All the above have caused me to have experiential knowledge in several areas of life's journey.

Finally, if we all live a clean, pure, holy, consecrated life before Jehovah God we are then able to say as is written in the following scripture:

Isaiah 61:1:3 (AMP):

"The Spirit of the Lord God is upon me, because the Lord has anointed and qualified me to preach the Gospel of good tidings to the meek, the poor, and afflicted; He has sent me to bind up and heal the brokenhearted, to proclaim liberty to the [physical and spiritual] captives and the opening of the prison and of the eyes to those who are bound,

To proclaim the acceptable year of the Lord [the year of His favor] and the day of vengeance of our God, to comfort all who mourn,

To grant [consolation and joy] to those who mourn in Zion — to give them an ornament (a garland or diadem) of beauty instead of ashes, the oil of joy instead of mourning, the garment [expressive] of praise instead of a heavy, burdened, and failing spirit — that they may be called oaks of righteousness [lofty, strong, and magnificent, distinguished for uprightness, justice, and right standing with God], the planting of the Lord, that He may be glorified."

*Have A Fruitful Life,
The Life That Can Only Be Found In Jesus Christ Our Lord And Savior, And Our Soon Coming King.*

DAILY CONFESSIONS

I Am Fearfuly And Wonderfully Made.

*No Good Thing Will He Withhold
From Those Who Walk Uprightly.*

I Am Redeemed By The Blood Of Jesus Christ.

I Am Accepted In The Beloved.

I Am A Joint Heir With Christ Jesus.

I Am A Royal Priesthood.

I Am The Apple Of God's Eye.

I Shall Live And Not Die.

Helen Patricia Rolle Rahming

*I Am The Righteousness Of God
In Christ Jesus.*

No Weapon Formed Against Me Shall Prosper.

I Am Born From Above And Not Beneath.

I Am Blessed Going In And Coming Out.

I Am An Overcomer.

If God Is For Me, Who Can Be Against Me.

I Am Accepted In The Beloved.

SPONSORS

I want to most graciously thank the following persons:

My son Edrick Neil Cleare and his wife Kimberley for financially sponsoring this book including the photographs.

My daughter Dr. Heatherlyn Hoffman and her husband Dr. Louis who also financially sponsored this book.

You have once again proven that you support my work by your continued financial contributions.

Printed in the United States
130902LV00006B/313-360/P